THE ARSENAL COMPANION

THE ARSENAL COMPANION

Gunners Anecdotes, History, Trivia, Facts & Figures

PAUL DONNELLEY

THE ARSENAL COMPANION

*Gunners Anecdotes, History,
Trivia, Facts & Figures*

All statistics, facts and figures are correct as of 1 August 2008

© Paul Donnelley

Paul Donnelley has asserted his rights in accordance with the Copyright, Designs
and Patents Act 1988 to be identified as the author of this work.

Published By:
Pitch Publishing (Brighton) Ltd
A2 Yeoman Gate
Yeoman Way
Durrington
BN13 3QZ

Email: info@pitchpublishing.co.uk
Web: www.pitchpublishing.co.uk

First published 2008

A catalogue record for this book is available from the British Library.

10-digit ISBN: 1-9054113-5-9
13-digit ISBN: 978-1-9054113-5-1

Printed and bound in Great Britain by Cromwell Press

Pour ma belle Karima

NOTE

Although commonly known as Highbury, Arsenal's home from 1913 until 2006 was officially called Arsenal Stadium. I have used the two names interchangeably. Since 2006, the club has played at the Emirates Stadium although some fans have insisted on calling the ground Ashburton Grove. For this book, I have referred to it exclusively as the Emirates Stadium. Facts and figures are correct up to 1 August 2008.

ABBREVIATIONS

ECC ....European Champions Cup
ECL .... European Champions League
ECWC .... European Cup Winners' Cup
ICFC .... Inter-Cities Fairs Cup
QF .... Quarter-finalists
SF ....Semi-finalists
UC .... Uefa Cup

INTRODUCTION

I have loved football all of my life and have many, many happy memories on the pitch and now watching and commentating on matches for television.

As I flick through this small book, I am reminded of the nine years I spent in an Arsenal shirt. It makes me think of winning the Fairs Cup, the first trophy at the club for 17 years, and then the next year when we won the club's first Double and Charlie George's unique way of celebrating his winning goal against Liverpool.

I had the privilege and honour of being Arsenal's captain, but it could have been so different for me. I was naturally upset when we lost two consecutive League Cup Finals and even asked for a transfer request. The great Bertie Mee persuaded me to stay and I am glad that he did. You can see the results of that discussion in this book.

I like football stories and this book has lots of anecdotes about a club that will always be part of me – it also has all the statistics about Arsenal that you could want. I will keep it by me for a fun read and I recommend you do the same.

Frank McLintock,
Arsenal FC, 1964-73

INTRODUCTION

Football teams – whatever the directors may think – belong to the fans. It's the people who sit in the stand each week who are the real lifeblood of the club. They don't change their loyalty. They don't sell their admiration. When the latest footballing superstar has moved on, they will still be there – cheering, groaning – sharing the team's highs and lows. Without them, highly paid players would be kicking a ball on pitches in empty stadia. The book you are holding in your hands was written by an Arsenal fan – someone who could not imagine spending time writing a book about another football team. I vividly remember my first time at Highbury and my first visit to the Emirates Stadium – oddly, the opponents on both those occasions wore blue shirts. At Highbury, I watched a defeat – Bertie Mee was the manager – but at the Emirates, under Arsène Wenger, I saw a comfortable win. Although Arsenal have not won a trophy for three years now under Mr Wenger, we have a team that is more than capable of winning more silverware for the Highbury House boardroom.

This small book adds to the ever-expanding literature about the greatest football team in the world. It contains facts, figures, trivia, funny stories and remembrances of good times and heartbreak. It has all the cup final teams and the results of every season since 1889-90. There are quotes about Arsenal and by representatives of the club, not to mention a few opponents.

I'd like to thank the following for their help, inspiration or kindness: Jeremy Beadle que tu dorme in paix, Paul Camillin, Tony Church, Gavin Fuller, Paul Gingell, Suzanne Kerins, Dominic Midgley, James Steen, Mitchell Symons, Nicola Wilson and Vince Wright.

I hope you enjoy *The Arsenal Companion* – I have had tremendous fun writing it. If you have any comments – bouquets or brickbats – I would love to hear from you, either via the publishers or my website.

Up the Gunners!

Paul Donnelley, 2008
www.pauldonnelley.com

WHAT'S IN A NAME?

Dial Square FC

The club's original name (after the location of a workshop in the munitions factory between Woolwich and Plumstead where the players worked) on Saturday 11 December 1886 when they played their first game winning 6-0 against Eastern Wanderers on a muddy pitch on the Isle of Dogs in east London.

Royal Arsenal

Fifteen members of Dial Square FC officially adopted the title of Royal Arsenal. The club was nicknamed the Royals. It is believed the name originates from the venue for a meeting on Christmas Day 1886 to discuss plans – The Royal Oak pub. The pub, near to Woolwich Arsenal station, later changed its name to The Pullman. In June 2005, construction began on the Docklands Light Railway extension to Woolwich Arsenal and the pub and several buildings nearby were demolished in 2007.

Woolwich Arsenal

The second name change occurred in 1891 when the club turned professional. However, the Football League continued to refer to the club as Royal Arsenal until 1896.

Arsenal

In 1913, through the machinations of chairman and owner Sir Henry Norris, Woolwich Arsenal moved to north London and on Friday 3 April 1914 dropped the geographical location from their name. For a time the club was known albeit unofficially as "The Arsenal" and some people still refer to it by that name. In 1926 Herbert Chapman insisted the club should drop the definite article.

THE THINGS THEY SAY – I

"One of the Derby chaps was heard to mutter: 'A journey to the molten interior of the earth's core would be rather more pleasant and comfortable an experience than our forthcoming visit to the Royal Arsenal.'"

Derby Post, 15 January 1891

SIX FOUNDING FATHERS

If anyone can be said to be the founding fathers of Arsenal, then the following six men could claim that title. It was their initiative that led to the formation of Dial Square FC in 1886.

David Danskin

Danskin was born at 11.30pm on Friday 9 January 1863 in Back Street (now Somerville Street), Burntisland, Fife and raised in Kirkaldy. He played for Kirkcaldy Wanderers alongside Jack McBean and Peter Connolly, two future Royal Arsenal colleagues. In 1885, searching for work, Danskin moved to London where he landed a job at the Dial Square workshop at the Royal Arsenal in Woolwich. It was Danskin who arranged a whip-round among his munitions factory colleagues to buy the team's first football. Fifteen men paid sixpence to join the club and Danskin added three shillings of his own money. He was captain for the first match against Eastern Wanderers and played for the club for the next two years, as they became Royal Arsenal. Danskin's footballing career was ended by an injury he picked up playing Clapton in January 1889. In 1892, Danskin stood for election to Woolwich Arsenal's committee but was not elected. He joined another works team and began to support Royal Ordnance Factories, but they folded in 1896. In 1907 he moved to Coventry and began working for the Standard Motor Company, but his football injuries forced another early retirement. Danskin died on Wednesday 4 August 1948, aged 85, at a Warwick hospice. He was buried in London Road Cemetery in Coventry, beside his first wife Georgina. On Monday 23 July 2007, The Arsenal Scotland Supporters Club unveiled a plaque to Danskin, near his birthplace.

Fred Beardsley

Arsenal's first goalie was born in Nottingham in 1856. He worked in a government munitions factory in Chilwell, playing football in his spare time. In 1884, he played in goal for Nottingham Forest in the FA Cup Semi-Final against Queen's Park and when the match went to a replay was sacked for taking time off without official permission. He moved to London to work at the Royal Arsenal. Beardsley kept a clean sheet in Arsenal's very first game but he also continued to play between the sticks for Nottingham Forest. It was during one of these visits home that Beardsley and Morris Bates managed to persuade Forest to donate a set of kit to the fledgling club. Beardsley played for 67 times – including the Royals' first FA Cup match, a qualifying game against Lyndhurst in 1889 and was between the sticks when Arsenal won the Kent Senior Cup and London Charity Shield in 1890. After he stopped playing, Beardsley was a director of Woolwich Arsenal until 1910, which included a spell as vice-chairman. He died at Plumstead in 1939 at the age of 82.

Morris Bates

Born in 1864, Joseph Morris Bates played 73 first-team matches for Royal Arsenal becoming club captain and leading the team to their first trophies: the Kent Senior Cup and London Charity Cup in 1890. He retired on a high but, for reasons unknown, severed all ties with the club. He died at Woolwich from tuberculosis on Wednesday 6 September 1905, aged 41.

Jack Humble

Elegantly bewhiskered John Wilkinson Humble was born at Hartburn, County Durham, in 1862. Aged 18, he moved to London with his brother to work at Royal Arsenal, walking the entire 400 miles. A keen football fan, it is not known if Humble ever actually played for an Arsenal team or was merely one of the backroom boys. It was Humble at the annual general meeting in 1891 held at the Windsor Castle Music Hall who suggested the club turn professional. He later joined the board – but in 1929, he was forced to resign in the scandal that brought down the chairman Sir Henry Norris. Although Humble had not done anything wrong, the FA decreed that he should have kept a closer eye on Norris's behaviour – perhaps easier said than done. He died in December 1931, aged 69.

Richard Pearce

A friend of David Danskin, with whom he worked at Dial Square.

Elijah Watkins

Another friend and colleague of Danskin, he became the club's first secretary. Of the club's first match on Saturday 11 December 1886, Watkins was to say, "Talk about a football pitch! This one eclipsed any I ever heard of or saw. I could not venture to say what shape it was, but it was bounded by backyards as to about two-thirds of the area, and the other portion was – I was going to say a ditch, but I think an open sewer would be more appropriate."

THE IRISH CONNECTION, 1977-78

Terry Neill

William John Terence Neill was born in Belfast, Northern Ireland on Friday 8 May 1942. He joined Arsenal in December 1959 and was the club's youngest captain and manager.

Pat Jennings, MBE, OBE

Born in Newry, County Down on Tuesday 12 June 1945, Jennings joined Arsenal on 11 August 1977. He did not receive a signing-on fee but a four-year contract worth £80,000.

Pat Rice

Born on St Patrick's Day 1949 in Belfast, Rice was raised in London and joined Arsenal as an apprentice in 1964. On Saturday 2 December 1967, he made his debut as a sub for George Graham in a 1-0 league defeat at Burnley. Three days later, on Tuesday 5 December 1967, he made his first start in the 2-1 League Cup victory, also against Burnley (albeit playing in the left-back position). Rice became right-back when Bertie Mee moved Peter Storey into midfield at the start of the first double-winning season. He was ever-present that season, and in 1971-72, 1975-76 and 1976-77. He became captain in 1977 and is the only player to appear in all five of the club's FA Cup Finals between 1971 and 1980. After 528 games and 13 goals, he left Highbury for Watford in 1980 – but returned as youth team coach in 1984. In 1996 he became Arsène Wenger's assistant.

Sammy Nelson

Born on April Fool's Day 1949 in Belfast, he signed for Arsenal on his 17th birthday in 1966. Nelson originally played on the left wing but Bertie Mee converted him to the left-back position where he understudied Bob McNab. His first-team debut was in a goalless draw against Ipswich Town at Highbury on Saturday 25 October 1969. On Tuesday 21 April 1970, he made his international debut against England as a sub but was still second fiddle to McNab at Arsenal. It wasn't until McNab left in 1975 that Sammy Nelson finally made the number three shirt his own. For the next five seasons he was the regular left-back. Following Kenny Sansom's arrival, Nelson signed for Brighton & Hove Albion in September 1981 for £10,000. In 339 games, Nelson scored a dozen times.

David O'Leary

Born in London, O'Leary represented the Republic of Ireland 68 times. He was at Arsenal for 20 years from 1973 to 1993 and played over 550 games, before moving to Leeds United – where he moved into management.

Frank Stapleton

A forward, Stapleton originally wanted to play for Manchester United but signed for Arsenal in June 1972. He made his first-team debut in the 1-1 draw against Stoke City on Saturday 29 March 1975 and when Malcolm Macdonald joined Arsenal the following year, the two of them made a great striking partnership – hitting the back of the net 46 times between them in 1976-77. Stapleton was Arsenal's top scorer for the next three seasons. In August 1981, he signed for Manchester United at a cost of £900,000 (the sum was set by a tribunal after the two clubs could not come to an agreement).

Liam Brady

"Chippy" Brady began his Arsenal career in 1970 signing schoolboy forms with the club and turning professional on his 17th birthday in 1973. He made his debut on Saturday 6 October 1973 as a substitute for Jeff Blockley in the 1-0 home win against Birmingham City. It was not until the 1974-75 season that Brady became a regular in the side. His brilliant ball control made him indispensable in midfield, and he was voted Arsenal's player of the year three times and chosen as the PFA Player of the Year in 1979. The following summer, he signed for Juventus for just over £500,000. Brady played more than 500 games for Arsenal at all levels and scored more than 100 goals.

John Devine

Born in Dublin on Tuesday 11 November 1958, John Anthony Devine joined Arsenal in November 1974 as an apprentice. He turned pro in 1976. A full-back, he preferred playing on the right and made his debut on Saturday 22 April 1978, in a 3-1 win over Leeds United. Devine played left-back in the 1980 FA Cup final but missed the Cup Winners' Cup Final with Valencia four days later. Injury blighted his last two years at Highbury and he only played 23 games. In 1981, he married Irish beauty queen Michelle Rocca – but they divorced in 1990. She is now the girlfriend of Van Morrison and has appeared on his album covers.

THE FRENCH CONNECTION, 2007-08

Arsène Wenger, OBE

Born at Strasbourg on Saturday 22 October 1949, Wenger officially joined Arsenal from the Japanese side Nagoya Grampas 8 on Tuesday 1 October 1996. His first match in charge was a 2-0 victory over Blackburn Rovers on Saturday 12 October 1996. He won the double for the club in his first full season in charge.

Abou Diaby

The midfielder signed for the Gunners from Auxerre on Friday 13 January 2006 for around £2m, making his debut eight days later in the 1-0 defeat by Everton. He wore the number two shirt in the 2007-08 season and made 20 appearances plus seven as sub and scored four goals.

William Gallas

Club captain Gallas, squad number ten, joined Arsenal from Chelsea on Thursday 31 August 2006 in the deal that took Ashley Cole to the west London club. In addition, Arsenal were paid £5million. In bitter recriminations following the deal, Chelsea issued a statement that Gallas had threatened to deliberately score own goals if he was not allowed to leave Stamford Bridge. Gallas rejected the Blues' claims and accused his old club of lacking class and "hiding behind false accusations". In 2007-08, Gallas played 42 times and scored four goals.

Mathieu Flamini

Flamini, who wore number 16 in 2007-08, played for Olympic Marseille but turned down a long-term contract to join Arsenal on Thursday 22 July 2004 for no transfer fee much to the annoyance of Marseille manager José Anigo who ranted, "This is a beautiful treason. He used me." Flamini hit back: "This is not a matter of money. I just didn't get on well with the manager and failed to reach an agreement. I realise that Marseille didn't really want to keep me and I was not their priority. All I can say is that I have always been very honest with the club who boosted my career. I just didn't manage to reach an agreement with them and this is very common in football." Flamini played 39 times for the Gunners in 2007-08 but on Tuesday 1 July 2008, he signed a four-year contract with AC Milan for £4million after Wenger refused to offer him more than £55,000-a-week.

Bacary Sagna

Like Diaby, Sagna, squad number three, joined Arsenal from Auxerre. He signed on Thursday 12 July 2007 and made his debut exactly one month later in the 2-1 victory over Fulham at the Emirates. He played 38 times for the club in 2007-08 and hit the back of the net once.

Lassana Diarra

He joined Arsenal on transfer deadline day Friday 31 August 2007 from rivals Chelsea for an undisclosed fee. He inherited the number eight shirt from Freddie Ljungberg who had joined West Ham. Diarra spent just five months at the Emirates, unhappy that he was not getting more first team action. In January 2008, he joined Portsmouth for about £5m.

Gaël Clichy

The left-back, squad number 22, joined the club on Monday 4 August 2003 from AS Cannes for £250,000. Clichy played 48 times for Arsenal in 2007-08 and made one appearance as substitute.

Armand Traoré

A defender, he joined the club on Tuesday 1 August 2006 from AS Monaco. In the 2007-08 season, he wore the number 30 shirt and made nine appearances plus two as substitute.

UP FOR THE CUP – I

Arsenal 0 Cardiff City 1

Arsenal's first cup final appearance was at Wembley for the FA Cup Final on Saturday 23 April 1927 against Cardiff City before 91,206 fans. Arsenal lost 1-0. It was the first and only time the FA Cup has left England and it was the infamous final when Arsenal goalie Dan Lewis seemed to have a shot from Cardiff's Hughie Ferguson covered only for it to slide into the goal off his shiny new jersey with just 16 minutes remaining. Since then every Arsenal goalkeeping jersey has been washed before it is worn. The BBC commentators for the match were Arsenal director (and future manager) George Allison and Derek McCulloch (later to become the children's entertainer Uncle Mac). Arsenal: Dan Lewis, Tom Parker (captain), Andy Kennedy, Alf Baker, Jack Butler, Bob John, Joe Hulme, Charles Buchan, Jimmy Brain, Billy Blyth, Sid Hoar.

THE FIVE SHORTEST MANAGERIAL SPELLS

Pat Rice – Two weeks

The Irish former right-back took over the reins for a fortnight (16-30 September 1996) awaiting Arsène Wenger's arrival at Highbury after the board sacked Bruce Rioch.

Steve Burtenshaw – Two months

Coach, chief scout and caretaker manager Steve Burtenshaw fulfilled many roles at Arsenal. He became coach in 1971 replacing Don Howe who went off to manage West Bromwich Albion. Both tenures lasted two years. Burtenshaw left Arsenal and became manager of Sheffield Wednesday, coach and caretaker manager of Everton and finally manager at Queens Park Rangers, He returned to Highbury as coach and scout and became caretaker manager after Don Howe resigned on Saturday 22 March 1986. Upon George Graham's appointment, Burtenshaw resumed his coaching duties. He left the club in 1996 to join Stewart Houston at Queens Park Rangers.

Joe Shaw – Five months

After his 15-year long playing career with the Gunners ended, Shaw became manager of the reserves. On Saturday 6 January 1934, following the unexpected death of Herbert Chapman, he took over the first team and led them to the completion of Chapman's hat-trick of championships. Following the appointment of George Allison as manager in June 1934, Shaw returned to the reserves. He later briefly became Chelsea coach but returned to Highbury in 1947 as assistant to Tom Whittaker. He finally retired in 1956 after almost fifty years at the club. Under him, Arsenal played 23 games and won 14, a 61 per cent success rate. He died in September 1963 at the age of 80.

Stewart Houston – Five months

The former Manchester United full-back had two spells as Arsenal manager – following the sackings of George Graham on Tuesday 21 February 1995 and Bruce Rioch just over a year later on Monday 12 August 1996. In his first spell in charge, he led the club to the final of the European Cup Winners' Cup only to see them lose to Real Zaragoza to a last minute looping goal from ex-Spurs player Nayim.

The performance was not enough to earn Houston a fulltime spell in the manager's chair and he became assistant to Bruce Rioch when he was appointed on Thursday 15 June 1995. When Rioch was fired, Houston again became caretaker while awaiting Arsène Wenger's arrival from Grampus Eight. Realising he was not going to get the job, apparently under any circumstances, Houston left Arsenal to become manager at Queens Park Rangers and, in a role reversal, appointed Rioch as his assistant. Houston did not have a happy time at Loftus Road and was sacked in November 1997. (Former Arsenal midfielder John Hollins became caretaker manager.) The following year he rejoined George Graham when the disgraced former Arsenal boss became manager of Spurs. When Graham was sacked in March 2001, Houston left White Hart Lane.

Thomas Mitchell – Seven months

Dumfries-born Mitchell became secretary-manager of Blackburn Rovers in 1884 and before he left in 1896 had seen his team win the FA Cup five times. In August 1897, he became Woolwich Arsenal's first professional manager. The pressure of running the club proved too much and he resigned in March 1898, as the team sat in fifth place in the Second Division. On his watch, Arsenal played 26 games, winning 14, a 53 per cent success rate.

THE THINGS THEY SAY – II

"Go back to Bradford and get a job. You will never make the grade as a professional footballer."

George Allison to Len Shackleton, April 1940

DON'T MENTION THE WAR

Arsenal's eccentric goalkeeper Jens Lehmann could amaze and infuriate fans in equal measure. He had a similar effect on his opponents and, if the story is correct, on his own team mates. One day he kept goal against Southampton and upset several of their players. As the match ended, the referee left the field with Patrick Vieira and commented, "They don't seem to like him, do they?" Vieira replied, perhaps humorously, "No, we don't like him either. He's German."

ON ME 'AD, SON

In the days before it became a given that professional sportsman could be used to advertise products unrelated to their sport, Denis Compton became the face of Brylcreem for many years. In the Seventies Charlie George was signed to promote eggs by the Egg Marketing Board. Little or no thought went into the campaign and unsurprisingly it flopped within a very short period. The ad had the slogan *E for B and Charlie George* which caused the North Bank favourite to comment later, "No one, myself included, had the foggiest bloody idea what 'E for B' actually stood for." Peter Marinello signed with great fanfare in January 1970 modelled for Freeman's catalogue, appeared on *Top of the Pops* with Pan's People, and starred in a poster campaign advertising milk. Charlie Nicholas put his name to all manner of items including tank tops, leather trousers, fitted kitchens, an all-leather white suit for Top Man and a range for men's clothing store Burtons. More recent campaigns have also featured Arsenal players. These have included John Hartson who advertised Advanced Hair Studio to help men who were balding. Thierry Henry promoted the Renault Clio – "Va-va-voom" (where he met his now ex-wife Claire Merry), Nike and Google's Joga Bonito social network plus various other Nike adverts and was one of Gillette's sporting champions (along with Roger Federer and Tiger Woods). Freddie Ljungberg posed in Calvin Klein underwear making him something of a gay icon. David Seaman and Ian Wright appeared in the Nike *Parklife* video and Wright was also in commercials for Chicken Tonight cooking sauce, Ladbrokes the bookies and computer game Wii. In 2008, Cesc Fàbregas appeared in videos for Pepsi and Nike.

THE THINGS THEY SAY – III

"[Sir Alex Ferguson] lost it completely in one TV interview and started having a go at Arsène Wenger, telling him to concentrate on talking to Ian Wright about his challenges. But I tell you what: when has he ever seen Ian Wright jump into the crowd and kick somebody? And believe me, I've had much more reason to do that than Eric Cantona. There's absolutely no way Cantona gets more stick than me. But that's typical United – they reckon the world is against them."

Ian Wright, 1997

THE COMPLETE MANAGERIAL RECORD

Name	From	To	P	W	D	L	F	A	%W
Sam Hollis	Aug 1894	Jul 1897	95	43	14	38	213	181	45.26
Thomas Mitchell	Aug 1897	Mar 1898	26	14	4	8	66	46	53.85
George Elcoat	Mar 1898	May 1899	43	23	6	14	92	55	53.49
Harry Bradshaw	Aug 1899	May 1904	189	96	39	54	329	173	50.79
Phil Kelso	Jul 1904	Feb 1908	151	63	31	57	225	228	41.27
George Morrell	Feb 1908	May 1915	294	104	73	117	365	412	35.37
Leslie Knighton	May 1919	Jun 1925	268	92	62	114	330	380	34.46
Herbert Chapman	Jun 1925	Jan 1934	403	201	97	105	864	598	49.88
Joe Shaw*	Jan 1934	Jun 1934	23	14	3	6	44	29	60.87
George Allison	Jun 1934	Jun 1947	283	131	75	77	543	333	46.29
Tom Whittaker	Jun 1947	Oct 1956	428	202	106	120	797	566	47.20
Jack Crayston	Oct 1956	May 1958	77	33	16	28	142	142	42.86

Name	From	To	P	W	D	L	F	A	%W
George Swindin	Jun 1958	May 1962	179	70	43	66	320	320	39.11
Billy Wright	May 1962	Jun 1966	182	70	43	69	336	330	38.46
Bertie Mee	Jun 1966	May 1976	539	241	148	150	739	542	44.71
Terry Neill	Jul 1976	Dec 1983	414	187	117	112	601	446	45.17
Don Howe	Dec 1983	Mar 1986	116	56	32	31	187	142	48.28
Steve Burtenshaw*	Mar 1986	May 1986	11	3	2	6	7	15	27.27
George Graham	May 1986	Feb 1995	460	225	133	102	711	403	48.91
Stewart Houston*	Feb 1995	Jun 1995	19	7	3	9	29	25	36.84
Bruce Rioch	Jun 1995	Aug 1996	47	22	15	10	67	37	46.81
Stewart Houston*	Aug 1996	Sep 1996	6	2	2	2	11	10	33.33
Pat Rice*	Sep 1996	Sep 1996	4	3	0	1	10	4	75.00
Arsène Wenger	Oct 1996		645	372	160	113	1166	581	57.67

* *Caretaker manager*

GUNNERS' NICKNAMES

Tony Adams – Rodders

The Arsenal captain supposedly has a resemblance to Rodney Trotter
(Nicholas Lyndhurst) in *Only Fools & Horses*.

Viv Anderson – Spider

The first black man to play for England, Anderson received his
nickname because of his gangling limbs.

Nicolas Anelka – The Incredible Sulk

The nickname came about after Anelka scored a first half hat-trick
against Leicester City on Saturday 20 February 1999 but
looked miserable for the entire second half.

Arsenal – The Royals

The club has also been known as the Woolwich Reds, the Bank
of England Club, the Gunners, and – following the famous
unbeaten Premiership season in 2003-04 – The Invincibles

Tommy Baldwin – Sponge

The man who left Highbury in the deal that brought
George Graham to the club was nicknamed Sponge
because his ability to soak up pressure.

Geoff Barnett – Marty

The extremely likeable but perennial reserve goalie was
nicknamed Marty because of his supposed resemblance
to the comedian Marty Feldman (1934-1982).

Júlio Baptista – The Beast

Baptista was nicknamed the Beast of Seville, and also The Tank.

Cliff Bastin – Boy Bastin

Bastin was just 17 when he arrived from Exeter in May 1929. In fact,
it is said that he looked so young that when he arrived at Arsenal
Stadium the commissionaire would not admit him thinking
he was only there to collect the autographs of the players.

Morris Bates – The Iron-Headed Man

A halfback, Bates was a former member of the Nottingham Forest team that donated a set of red shirts to Arsenal. Bates was able to head the ball, described by one author as "then virtually the weight of a cannonball", half the length of the pitch, hence his nickname.

Liam Brady – Chippy

Brady earned his nickname not because of his ability to chip the ball, but because of his liking for fried potatoes.

Gus Caesar – The Five-Minute Man

In 1987-88 he appeared mainly as a sub.

Jimmy Carter – Sanjay

So called because of his love of Indian food.

Herbert Chapman – Yorkshire's Napoleon

The first great Arsenal manager – and former Huddersfield boss – got his nickname from the newspaper *The Examiner*.

Wilf Copping – Iron Man

A 1930s hard man, Copping received his nickname because of his tenacity on the pitch. He was signed by Arsenal in June 1934 for £8,000, as a replacement for Bob John.

Ray Daniel – Bebe

After the American film, radio and television star Bebe Daniels.

Malcolm Macdonald – Supermac

Arrogant beyond belief on the pitch, but in fairness to Macdonald he managed to live up to his own hype.

Terry Mancini – Henry

The bald centre-half was named after the American composer.

Joe Murphy – The Judge

Murphy earned his nom-de-sport because remarkably he always wore a wig whenever he played!

THE ARSENAL – DECADE BY DECADE: 1890s

1889-90
FA Cup: Fourth qualifying round

1890-91
FA Cup: First round

1891-92
FA Cup: First round

1892-93
FA Cup: First round

1893-94

Second Division	P	W	D	L	F	A	W	D	L	F	A	Pts
9. Arsenal	28	9	1	4	33	19	3	3	8	19	36	28

FA Cup: First round

1894-95

Second Division	P	W	D	L	F	A	W	D	L	F	A	Pts
8. Arsenal	30	11	3	1	54	20	3	3	9	21	38	34

FA Cup: First round

1895-96

Second Division	P	W	D	L	F	A	W	D	L	F	A	Pts
7. Arsenal	30	11	1	3	43	11	3	3	9	16	31	32

FA Cup: First round

1896-97

Second Division	P	W	D	L	F	A	W	D	L	F	A	Pts
10. Arsenal	30	10	1	4	42	20	3	3	9	26	50	30

FA Cup: Fifth qualifying round

1897-98

Second Division	P	W	D	L	F	A	W	D	L	F	A	Pts
5. Arsenal	30	10	4	1	41	14	6	1	8	28	35	37

FA Cup: First round

1898-99

Second Division	P	W	D	L	F	A	W	D	L	F	A	Pts
7. Arsenal	34	14	2	1	55	10	4	3	10	17	31	41

FA Cup: First round

1899-1900

Second Division	P	W	D	L	F	A	W	D	L	F	A	Pts
8. Arsenal	34	13	1	3	47	12	3	3	11	14	31	36

FA Cup: Third qualifying round

Arsenal did not enter the Football League until 1893

UP FOR THE CUP – II

Arsenal 2 Huddersfield Town 0

Arsenal's second cup final and the first time they won the FA Cup in their 44-year history. When Herbert Chapman joined the club he had promised it would take five years to achieve success and this cup final was played almost five years to the day since he arrived at Highbury. Nine of the 11 players had been his signings. The Arsenal beat Huddersfield Town 2-0 at Wembley before 92,488 spectators on Saturday 26 April 1930. On the team bus to the game Arsenal goalie Charlie Preedy (replacing the injured and unfortunate Dan Lewis) had said to his team mates, "I know you think I'm the worst goalkeeper in the world. I probably am, but today I'm going to play like I'm the best." The match was watched by HM King George V, making his first public appearance in 18 months after an illness. BBC commentary was by Arsenal director George Allison. On 16 minutes Alex James opened the scoring putting the ball into the bottom corner of Huddersfield goalie Turner's net. With Arsenal one up, the LZ127 Graf Zeppelin flew over the stadium. The engine noise made the fans look up and distracted them from the game. It was only when the aircraft dipped its nose perhaps in salute that the crowd broke into a round of applause and cheers although reportedly some booed. The second half was rather scrappier than the first but Jack Lambert scored Arsenal's second to guarantee their name on the trophy. Arsenal: Charlie Preedy, Tom Parker (captain), Eddie Hapgood, Alf Baker, Bill Seddon, Bob John, Joe Hulme, David Jack, Jack Lambert, Alex James, Cliff Bastin.

THE THINGS THEY SAY – IV

"He was a real gentleman. He was not a soccer tactician by any stretch of the imagination, but he was always willing to listen to his players and he surrounded himself with good coaches. He let them sort out the tactics – he got on with running the club. And he did it brilliantly."

Alan Ball on Bertie Mee

UP FOR THE CUP – III

Arsenal 1 Newcastle United 2

Arsenal's third visit to Wembley for the FA Cup Final occurred on Saturday 23 April 1932 before 92,298 fans. Bob John opened the scoring with a header after 15 minutes but Newcastle United hit the back of the Arsenal net twice, the first in controversial circumstances. With seven minutes remaining in the first half, Jimmy Richardson of the Magpies chased a long pass and took the ball over the Arsenal dead ball line. The Gunners waited for the linesman to flag for a goal kick but he kept his flag down. Richardson crossed the ball and Jack Allen equalized with a header. The referee, Mr W. P. Harper, allowed the goal to stand even though he was unsighted more than 20 yards from the incident. Newsreels later showed that the ball was out and the goal should have been disallowed. After 72 minutes, Allen scored a second and the cup was on its way to Tyneside. Arsenal were the first team to score first at Wembley and still lose. Arsenal: Frank Moss, Tom Parker (captain), Eddie Hapgood, Charlie Jones, Herbie Roberts, George Male, Joe Hulme, David Jack, Jack Lambert, Cliff Bastin, Bob John.

NETIQUETTE

In the summer of 2000, explosive winger and double-winner Marc Overmars left Arsenal for Barcelona with the Spanish giants paying the Gunners a massive fee of £25million (€39.6million). The move from north London to the Nou Camp meant Overmars became the most expensive Dutch footballer of all time. Oddly, it was also the first transfer in football history to be announced on a player's own individual website.

MORE GUNNERS' NICKNAMES

Arsenal player and boss George Graham was known as Stroller because of his languid style of play on the pitch. Off it he was known by the lesser-known nickname of The Peacock because of his sartorial elegance. When he returned to the club as manager, he was known as Gadaffi or Ayatollah – a less than complimentary nicknames bestowed (behind his back) by some of his players. A selection of other Arsenal players' nicknames are:

Eddie Clamp..Chopper
Leslie Compton ....Big Leslie/Big 'Ead
Joe Baker.............................The Laughing Cavalier
Jack Crayston ....Gentleman Jack
John Flanagan ....Little Jack
Marc Overmars...Roadrunner
Ray Parlour...Romford Pele
Charlie Preedy...Spider
Herbie Roberts.. Policeman
David Rocastle ....Rocky
Ehud Rogers ....Tim
Tomáš Rosický ....The Footballing Mozart
David Seaman.. Safe Hands
Alan Skirton....................The Highbury Express/Fish
Peter Storey....................................Snouty/Cold Eyes
Bobby Templeton..............The Prince of Dribblers

Marc "Roadrunner" Overmars – the Dutch flying winger was named after the cartoon character because of his speed – gave Parlour the nickname of Romford Pelse. Ehud Rogers was called Tim by his teammates because they could not pronounce his Christian name. While 1970s hard man Peter Storey got the moniker Cold Eyes because it was said that a look from Storey could chill an opponent's marrow at 30 paces. Team mate Alan Hudson said, "Before a game his eyes would become fixated on the walls, or the ceiling. You'd look at the eyes and think, 'Oh my God, what's in his head?' His expression was so eerie. It was like looking at Hannibal Lecter in *The Silence of the Lambs*."

THE RIVALS – ARSENAL v LIVERPOOL

Liverpool dominated English football for much of the Seventies and Eighties yet Arsenal still managed to trip them up on several occasions during that period. It was against Liverpool that Arsenal first wore red shirts with white sleeves (on Saturday 4 March 1933). Here are some remarkable matches between the two teams.

Arsenal 8 Liverpool 1 – 1 September 1934

The first home game of a season which eventually resulted in Arsenal's third consecutive league title was watched by 54,062 fans. Before the match kicked off the band played 'Twenty One Today' as it was almost 21 years to the day that Woolwich Arsenal played their first match at Highbury. Pundits and experts in the crowd expected a tight match – Arsenal had a cracking forward line-up but Liverpool had a great goalie in Arthur Riley. On 20 minutes Ray Bowden scored the first for the Gunners and then Ted Drake had a goal disallowed. Never one to be disheartened Drake soon made it 2-0 and that was the way it stayed at half-time. In the second half Jack Crayston scored his first goal at Highbury before Drake converted a corner from Pat Beasley. Alf Hanson scored Liverpool's solitary effort to make it 4-1. Cliff Bastin made it five before Bowden and Drake completed their hat-tricks. *The Times* reporter said, "The result… will make other clubs… wonder what hopes they can have of finishing ahead of Arsenal." Arsenal: Frank Moss, George Male, Eddie Hapgood (captain), Jack Crayston, Herbie Roberts, Wilf Copping, Pat Beasley, Ray Bowden, Ted Drake, Alex James, Cliff Bastin.

Liverpool 1 Arsenal 5 – 15 November 1952

Arsenal recorded their biggest-ever league victory at Anfield on the way to winning the First Division title. The Merseysiders took the lead through Jimmy Payne's right foot. Ben Marden equalised but it was not until the 52nd minute that Arsenal took the lead. Cliff Holton scored twice within four minutes. Marden added a second while Holton scored his hat-trick. Liverpool eventually avoided relegation by a single point. Arsenal: Jack Kelsey, John Chenhall, Joe Wade, Alex Forbes, Ray Daniel, Joe Mercer (captain), Arthur Milton, Jimmy Logie, Cliff Holton, Doug Lishman, Ben Marden.

Arsenal 2 Liverpool 1 (aet) – 8 May 1971

The FA Cup Final win that gave Arsenal their first double triumph was played on a blazing hot day before the usual Wembley sell-out crowd. After 90 minutes, the scores were level with neither team able to break the deadlock and referee Norman Burtenshaw blew the whistle to signal the end of the game. Coaches, trainers and managers spilled onto the pitch to give advice, encouragement and anything else they could think of. Two minutes into the first period of extra time Steve Heighway, Liverpool's number nine, broke through Arsenal's defences and put the ball past Bob Wilson who had come too far out of his goal in anticipation of a cross. Liverpool had only conceded one goal in the competition up to the final, so Arsenal's double dreams looked in tatters. However, Bertie Mee had not spent the previous five years instilling a never say die attitude and discipline in his team for nothing. Arsenal picked themselves up and Eddie Kelly scored the vital equaliser (George Graham also claimed the credit) after 101 minutes. Both sets of players showed signs of extreme exhaustion until with nine minutes left on the clock, Charlie George got the ball twenty yards from Ray Clemence's goal and let fly with a shot that gave the Liverpool and future England goalie no chance. The North Bank hero lay flat on his back until his delighted teammates mobbed him. Arsenal had completed the first double in their history. Arsenal: Bob Wilson, Pat Rice, Bob McNab, Peter Storey (Eddie Kelly), Frank McLintock (captain), Peter Simpson, George Armstrong, George Graham, John Radford, Ray Kennedy, Charlie George.

Liverpool 0 Arsenal 2 – 26 May 1989

To win George Graham his first championship as manager – and the club's first since the double season of 1970-71 – Arsenal had to go to Anfield and win by two clear goals which was a tall order at the best of times. If Arsenal didn't get that two-goal gap, the championship would go to Merseyside once again. Most neutrals did not give Arsenal a hope and fully expected Kenny Dalglish's men to gain a second double in four seasons. After all, Arsenal had not won at Anfield since 1974-75. To add extra pressure the match had been cancelled a month earlier because of the Hillsborough tragedy and the kick-off was delayed to ensure that the Arsenal fans got into Anfield. George Graham told his players that he would be happy if the half-time score was 0-0 and the team played in an unusual 5-3-2 formation. Perhaps unsurprisingly for a Graham side, at half time the score was indeed 0-0. Seven minutes into the second half, Nigel Winterburn crossed and Alan Smith opened Arsenal's account with a header. However, the referee consulted with his linesman before allowing the goal, after the Liverpool team claimed that the goal should not stand because Smith was either offside or had not touched the ball from the indirect free kick. Or was it something else? With ten minutes remaining, Michael Thomas was clear on goal but missed, hitting the ball straight at Bruce Grobbelaar in the Liverpool goal. The clock ticked down, seemed as if Arsenal wouldn't win by a big enough margin. In injury time, Lukic threw the ball to Dixon… Over to ITV's legendary commentator Brian Moore, "Arsenal come streaming forward now, in what surely will be their last attack… A good ball from Dixon, finding Smith, to Thomas, charging through midfield… Thomas… it's up for grabs now!... THOMAS! Right at the end…" From the kick-off Liverpool surged forward. Right-back Lee Dixon had tears in his eyes with the emotion and later said that he was hoping Liverpool attacked on the other flank because he could not see properly. The referee blew for time and Arsenal won the title. George Graham was named manager of the year. Arsenal: John Lukic, Lee Dixon, Nigel Winterburn, Michael Thomas, David O'Leary, Tony Adams (captain), David Rocastle, Kevin Richardson, Alan Smith, Steve Bould (Perry Groves), Paul Merson (Martin Hayes).

Arsenal 4 Liverpool 2 – 9 April 2004

At the start of April 2004 Arsenal were in contention to win the Champions League, the FA Cup and the Premier League However, when Liverpool came to Highbury the dreams of the Treble were in tatters. Manchester United knocked them out of the FA Cup and Chelsea did for the club in the Champions League. Now Arsenal were battling to protect an unbeaten record in the league (and become the first team since Preston North End in 1888-89 to go a whole season unbeaten) and an attempt to win the title. Things seem to go from bad to worse for the Gunners when Liverpool went in at half-time 2-1 ahead – but a hat-trick by Thierry Henry and a goal from Robert Pirès confirmed Arsenal's victory. Gerard Houllier, the Liverpool manager, said, "They showed why they are unbeaten in the league." Arsenal: Jens Lehmann, Lauren, Ashley Cole, Patrick Vieira (captain), Sol Campbell, Kolo Touré, Gilberto, Freddie Ljungberg (Martin Keown), Robert Pirès (Edu), Thierry Henry, Dennis Bergkamp.

Liverpool 3 Arsenal 6 – 9 January 2006

A League Cup quarter-final: Arsenal away to Liverpool – and a daunting task for Arsène Wenger's young side, but a great start saw Kolo Touré set up Jérémie Aliadière for the first goal. Robbie Fowler equalised but Arsenal were in no mood to surrender. Júlio Baptista hit two and Alex Song Billong one to make the score 4-1 to the Gunners at half time. In the second half Jerzy Dudek saved a Baptista penalty after Sami Hyypia had brought down Aliadière but the Beast scored two more. Consolation goals came from Steven Gerrard and Hyypia but it was Arsenal's night. It was the first time in nearly 80 years that Liverpool had conceded six goals at home and it was Arsenal's first League Cup win at Anfield. The match set up a semi-final clash with Tottenham Hotspur. Arsenal: Manuel Almunia, Justin Hoyte, Armand Traoré (Matthew Connolly), Theo Walcott (Abou Diaby), Kolo Touré (captain), Johan Djourou-Gbadjere, Cesc Fàbregas, Alexandre Song Billong, Denílson, Júlio Baptista, Jérémie Aliadière.

Liverpool 4 Arsenal 2 – 8 April 2008

The two teams met for the third time in six days. The first match was the first-leg of the Champions League Quarter-Final at the Emirates on Wednesday 2 April 2008 ended 1-1. Three days later, the two teams met again at the Emirates in the Premier League and again the score was 1-1. This third meeting – the second leg of the Champions League Quarter-Final – was the only one held at Anfield. With 13 minutes on the clock Abou Diaby scored the all-important away goal to put Arsenal into the lead. On the half-hour, Sami Hyypia headed a corner from Steven Gerrard into the Arsenal net and that was the way it stayed at half time. On 69 minutes, Fernando Torres put Liverpool 2-1 up and three minutes later Wenger made two substitutions for Arsenal replacing Flamini and Eboué. With just six minutes to go, Adebayor popped up with an equaliser for the Gunners – his 25th strike of the season. Away goals counting double Arsenal were on their way into the semis – for a whole minute. That was the time it took for Ryan Babel to be "fouled" by Kolo Touré and Gerrard to convert the penalty. In time added on, Babel added a fourth to wreck Arsenal's dreams of a place in the final. Arsenal: Manuel Almunia, Kolo Touré, Gaël Clichy, Emmanuel Eboué (Theo Walcott), William Gallas (captain), Philippe Senderos, Cesc Fàbregas, Alexander Hleb, Matthieu Flamini (Gilberto), Emmanuel Adebayor, Abou Diaby (Robin van Persie).

THE THINGS THEY SAY – V

"Go back to Bradford and get a job. You will never make the grade as a professional footballer."

George Allison to Len Shackleton, April 1940

GIANT-KILLERS

On two occasions, Arsenal have lost to Walsall in cup competitions. On Saturday 14 January 1933, Arsenal travelled to Fellows Park to play a Walsall side in poor form in the Third Division North. Herbert Chapman underestimated the minnows, resting several first team players while others were unavailable because of a flu epidemic. The Walsall team cost just £69 to assemble, compared to Arsenal, who spent £30,000 on their side. Chapman brought in left-back Tommy Black, left-half Norman Sidey, outside-right Billy Warnes and centre-forward Charlie Walsh. Of these only Sidey had played for the first-team before. It was claimed that Walsh was so fraught with nerves that he put one of his boots on before his sock, then on the pitch he missed a sitter and 'tackled' David Jack as he was about to shoot. Tommy Black had a running battle with a Walsall forward, finally lost his temper and hacked him down conceding a penalty that Bill Sheppard converted. Gilbert Alsop also scored giving the Saddlers a 2-0 win in front of a crowd of 11,150. Chapman was magnanimous telling the players, "Never mind boys, these things do happen." Cliff Bastin said, "Napoleon must have felt like that in Russia 120 years before." On the following Monday, having had the weekend to ruminate on the humiliation, Herbert Chapman called Black to his office and told him that he'd never play for Arsenal again and sold him to Plymouth Argyle a few days later. The cup match was his only first-team appearance. Charlie Walsh left for Brentford a fortnight later. The Arsenal team was: Frank Moss, George Male, Tommy Black, Frank Hill, Herbie Roberts, Norman Sidey, Billy Warnes, David Jack, Charlie Walsh, Alex James, Cliff Bastin. Fifty-one years later, history repeated itself. On Thursday 29 November 1984, Walsall played Arsenal in the fourth round of the League Cup. The Saddlers were again victorious, winning 2-1 for their first victory at Highbury in nine attempts. Stewart Robson got Arsenal's goal before a crowd of 22,406. Arsenal: Pat Jennings, Stewart Robson, Kenny Sansom, Chris Whyte, David O'Leary, Colin Hill, Alan Sunderland, Paul Davis, Tony Woodcock, Charlie Nicholas, Ian Allinson.

THE ARSENAL – DECADE BY DECADE: 1900s

1900-01

Second Division	P	W	D	L	F	A	W	D	L	F	A	Pts
7. Arsenal	34	13	3	1	30	11	2	3	12	9	24	36

FA Cup: Second round

1901-02

Second Division	P	W	D	L	F	A	W	D	L	F	A	Pts
4. Arsenal	34	13	2	2	35	9	5	4	8	15	17	42

FA Cup: First round

1902-03

Second Division	P	W	D	L	F	A	W	D	L	F	A	Pts
3. Arsenal	34	14	2	1	46	9	6	6	5	20	21	48

FA Cup: First round

1903-04

Second Division	P	W	D	L	F	A	W	D	L	F	A	Pts
2. Arsenal	34	15	2	0	67	5	6	5	6	24	17	49

FA Cup: Second round

1904-05

First Division	P	W	D	L	F	A	W	D	L	F	A	Pts
10. Arsenal	34	9	5	3	19	12	3	4	10	17	28	33

FA Cup: First round

1905-06

First Division	P	W	D	L	F	A	W	D	L	F	A	Pts
12. Arsenal	38	12	4	3	43	21	3	3	13	19	43	37

FA Cup: Semi-final

1906-07

First Division	P	W	D	L	F	A	W	D	L	F	A	Pts
7. Arsenal	38	15	1	3	38	15	5	3	11	28	44	44

FA Cup: Semi-final

1907-08

First Division	P	W	D	L	F	A	W	D	L	F	A	Pts
15. Arsenal	38	9	8	2	32	18	3	4	12	19	45	36

FA Cup: First round

1908-09

First Division	P	W	D	L	F	A	W	D	L	F	A	Pts
6. Arsenal	38	9	3	7	24	18	5	7	7	28	31	38

FA Cup: Second round

1909-10

First Division	P	W	D	L	F	A	W	D	L	F	A	Pts
18. Arsenal	38	6	5	8	17	19	5	4	10	20	48	31

FA Cup: Second round

CHRISTMAS DAY

Christmas Day Football League games were regular fixtures until the 1950s, but when Woolwich Arsenal moved to Highbury, it was with an undertaking that they would not play any matches on Christmas Day or Good Friday. However, the promise was broken not long after the club moved in. These are those Christmas Day contests – pre- and post- Highbury.

1894 ....Woolwich Arsenal 7 Port Vale 0
1895 ....Woolwich Arsenal 2 Port Vale 1
1896 ....Woolwich Arsenal 6 Lincoln City 2
1901 ....Woolwich Arsenal 0 Blackpool 0
1903 ....Woolwich Arsenal 4 Bradford City 1
1905 ....Woolwich Arsenal 4 Newcastle United 3
1907 ....Woolwich Arsenal 2 Newcastle United 2
1909 ....Woolwich Arsenal 0 Newcastle United 3
1912 ....Woolwich Arsenal 0 Notts County 0
1925 ....Arsenal 3 Notts County 0
1934 ....Arsenal 5 Preston North End 3
1936 ....Arsenal 4 Preston North End 1
1946 ....Arsenal 2 Portsmouth 1
1948 ....Arsenal 3 Derby County 3
1950 ....Arsenal 0 Stoke City 3
1951 ....Arsenal 4 Portsmouth 1
1954 ....Arsenal 1 Chelsea 0

THE THINGS THEY SAY – VI

"Normally his football is based on an offensive, passing game but he [can] fight for the team as well. That's a great sign – a sign of a winner."

Club captain William Gallas
on Cesc Fàbregas's spirit, 2008

THE FIRST TEAMS

Dial Square

Dial Square played their very first match on Saturday 11 December 1886 against Eastern Wanderers and ran out 6-0 winners. Dial Square: (probable) Beardsley, Danskin, Porteous, Gregory, Bee, Wolfe, Smith, Moy, Whitehead, Morris, Duggan.

Royal Arsenal

The first match under the name Royal Arsenal was played against Erith at Plumstead Common on Saturday 8 January 1887. Royal Arsenal: Beardsley, Danskin, Porteous, Gregory, Price, Wells, Smith, Moy, Whitehead, Crighton, Bee.

Woolwich Arsenal

The first match played by Woolwich Arsenal in the football league was on Saturday 2 September 1893 against Newcastle United at the Manor Ground, Plumstead, before a crowd of 10,000. At one stage Woolwich Arsenal were leading 2-0 with goals from Shaw and Elliott but in the last 15 minutes Newcastle pulled two back to earn a draw. Woolwich Arsenal: Charlie Williams, Joe Powell (captain), Bill Jeffrey, Daniel Devine, Bob Buist, David Howat, Duncan Gemmell, Jim Henderson, Walter Shaw, Arthur Elliott, Charlie Booth.

Highbury

The first match played at Highbury was on Saturday 6 September 1913 against Leicester Fosse in front of 20,000 fans. Leicester Fosse's Tommy Benfield scored the first goal at the new stadium but George Jobey equalised to score the first Arsenal goal. However, the pitch had not been finished and had a distinctive slope. There was no warm water in the dressing rooms and when Jobey was injured, he had to be taken to the dressing room on a milk cart. A late penalty from Archibald Devine meant the ten-man Gunners ran out 2-1 winners. (Serving his country, Sergeant Tommy Benfield of the 6th Battalion of the Leicestershire Regiment was killed aged 29 by a German sniper on 19 September 1918). Woolwich Arsenal: Joe Lievesley, Joe Shaw, Joe Fidler, George Grant, Percy Sands, Angus McKinnon, David Greenaway, Wally Hardinge, George Jobey, Archibald Devine, Tom Winship.

Emirates

The first game at the Emirates Stadium was Dennis Bergkamp's testimonial against Ajax on Saturday 22 July 2006. Arsenal won 2-1 and the first-half side was made up of current players, with the second-half side a team of Arsenal veterans. Thierry Henry and Nwankwo Kanu got the Gunners goals. First-half: Manuel Almunia, Justin Hoyte, Pascal Cygan, Matthew Connolly, Armand Traoré, Alexander Hleb, Alexandre Song Billong, Mathieu Flamini, Ryan Smith, Dennis Bergkamp, Jérémie Aliadière. Substitutes: Mart Poom, Sebastian Larsson, Nicklas Bendtner, Fabrice Muamba, Joe O'Cearuill, Mark Randall, Vincent Van den Berg, Arturo Lupoli, Anthony Stokes. Second-half: David Seaman, Lee Dixon, Nigel Winterburn, Steve Bould, Gilles Grimandi, Marc Overmars, Emmanuel Petit, Edu, Ray Parlour, Dennis Bergkamp, Thierry Henry, Ian Wright, Oleg Luzhny, Giovanni van Bronckhorst, Alex Manninger, Patrick Vieira, Glenn Helder, Nwankwo Kanu. The first League match was on Saturday 19 August 2006 against Aston Villa. The game ended 1-1 and Gilberto Silva scored Arsenal's goal. Arsenal: Jens Lehmann, Emmanuel Eboué, Justin Hoyte (Mathieu Flamini), Johan Djourou-Gbadjere, Alexander Hleb, Cesc Fàbregas, Gilberto Silva, Freddie Ljungberg (Theo Walcott), Emmanuel Adebayor (Robin van Persie), Thierry Henry.

UP FOR THE CUP – IV

Arsenal 1 Sheffield United 0

Back to Wembley for the third time in the 1930s, this time Arsenal's opponents were Sheffield United on Saturday 25 April 1936. It was the only FA Cup Final attended by HM King Edward VIII during his short reign, which ended in December of the same year with his abdication. Ninety-three thousand, three hundred and eighty-four fans saw Ted Drake score the only goal of the game 15 minutes from time as Arsenal won their second FA Cup six years after their first triumph. In the league Arsenal had finished sixth so the FA Cup was their only chance of glory. In a reverse of Arsène Wenger's League Cup policy manager George Allison rested his best players in the league and kept his strongest team for the cup. It resulted in a fine of £250 for the club by the Football League. Remarkably there were no newsreel cameras to capture the events. Arsenal: Alex Wilson, George Male, Eddie Hapgood, Jack Crayston, Herbie Roberts, Wilf Copping, Joe Hulme, Ray Bowden, Ted Drake, Alex James (captain), Cliff Bastin.

THE THINGS THEY SAY – VII

"It depends what you compare. If you want to count the number of championships Ferguson has won and [Brian] Clough has won, you cannot compare. So what Bob Paisley has won and how long Bob Paisley has been in charge and Ferguson, you cannot compare. All together nobody has done better."

*Arsène Wenger on whether Alex Ferguson is
one of the top managers of all time, 2006.*

ARSENAL SONGS

Should you be so inclined there is a CD available to buy (on the Cherry Red label) called *Highbury Anthems*, which features "18 Gooner Classics". The track listing is as follows:

1..Arsenal Number 1 – Arsenal FC 2000
2...Hot Stuff – Arsenal FC 1998
3..One Nil To The Arsenal – Sweet FA
4...Ooh Ooh Tony Adams – A-Team
5..............................We Will Follow The Arsenal – Sean Gunnery
6...................................Vieira – Jackin' The Box & DJ Fresh
7..We Are Arsenal – Various Artists
8..Super Arsenal FC – Arsenal FC 1979
9...Thierry Henry – Arsène Sings
10...................................... Official Arsenal March – Arsenal Choir
11... Mr Bergkamp – Yeah
12..................We're Back (Where We Belong) – Arsenal FC 1989
13............................Shouting For The Gunners – Arsenal FC 1993
14.. Come On You Reds – Arsenal Choir
15..Highbury Sunshine – Yeah
16..................................Only Cockney Rebel... – Halftime Oranges
17....................................Up With The Arsenal – Arsenal FC 1972
18... Good Old Arsenal – Arsenal FC

'Arsenal Number 1' – which is sung to the tune of 'Mambo No.5 (A Little Bit Of…)' by Lou Bega – reached number 46 in the UK charts during a one-week stay. 'Hot Stuff' was the club's official song for the

1998 FA Cup Final and was based on Donna Summers's disco smash hit of the same name. It was also the most successful Arsenal song in the club's history spending five weeks on the chart and peaking at number nine. 'Shouting For The Gunners' was the official 1993 FA Cup Final song and featured Tippa Irie and Peter Hunnigale. It spent three weeks on the chart and reached number 34. Former footballer turned TV pundit Jimmy Hill wrote the lyrics to 'Good Old Arsenal' , which uses the tune of 'Rule Britannia'. There was a television competition to write lyrics for an Arsenal song but it failed to produce anything worthwhile so Hill approached Bertie Mee and asked if he could submit an idea. It spent seven weeks on the chart and reached number 16.

If *Highbury Anthems* isn't enough to sate your musical appetite, then another Arsenal CD which is also available to purchase is *Good Old Arsenal* (also on the Cherry Red label) by Arsenal FC and Supporters. Its full 20-track listing is as follows:

1	Good Old Arsenal
2	Roll out the Red Carpet
3	Come On You Gunners
4	Boys from Highbury
5	I Wish I Could Play Like Charlie George
6	Kings of London
7	Highbury Sunshine
8	The Gus Caesar Rap
9	One Night at Anfield
10	The Charlie George Calypso
11	Gooneroonie
12	Highbury Heartbeat
13	Arsenal Rap
14	Here We Go Again
15	Ooh Ooh Tony Adams
16	We are the Best
17	Arriverdici (sic) Liam
18	Arsenal
19	The Victory Song
20	Arsenal, We're On Your Side

And still there is *We Love You Arsenal* (released on Sanctuary Records) and its track listing is as follows:

1 .... The Arsène Wenger Chorus
2 .... Come On You Reds
3 .... Boys From Highbury
4 ....(Been A Gunner) Since '79
5 .... They Think It's All Over
6 .... Arsène Wenger On Bass
7 .... We Love You Arsenal (We Do)
8 .... Nuff Love (To The Arsenal)
9 .... Tom Hark
10 .... Jose Antonio
11 .... Carmina Burana
12 .... Stand Up For The Arsenal
13 .... We've Got Dennis Bergkamp
14 .... All About The Arsenal
15 .... The Gooner Chillout
16 .... The Season (03/04)
17 .... Good Old Arsenal
18 .... (Been A Gunner) Since '79 – Replay AET

In the early 1970s, Charlie George tried to jump on the glam rock bandwagon by recording a (thankfully) one-off novelty song under the name Charlie Gorgeous. The record, 'A Love Song For My Lady', was never released. On Saturday 28 August 1993, Ian Wright entered the charts with his song 'Do The Wright Thing', which peaked at number 43.

THE THINGS THEY SAY – VIII

"I sensed there was a special soul in the stadium because it is a little bit strange and you cannot have that feeling anywhere else. I feel that part of my own soul is there. When you first arrive at Highbury you do not expect it – you are saying, 'Where is the stadium? Where is the stadium?' And then suddenly you are in front of it. It is in the middle of the city. It is something I love about English football. A stadium that sits among the streets of houses."

Arsène Wenger on why Highbury was special.

UP FOR THE CUP – V

Arsenal 2 Liverpool 0

It was 14 years and four days before Arsenal returned to Wembley for the FA Cup Final. This time their opponents were Liverpool on Saturday 29 April 1950. The boys from Anfield were no match for the men from Highbury and Arsenal ran out 2-0 winners with both goals coming from Reg Lewis, one either side of half time. The attendance was 100,000 fans. Both teams changed their kit for the match – Arsenal wore gold shirts and white shorts while Liverpool wore white shirts and black shorts. Incredibly, Arsenal captain trained with the Liverpool team in the run-up to the final – he had a greengrocer's business in Wallasey. His Arsenal team-mates travelled to Brighton to take the air. Arsenal: George Swindin, Laurie Scott, Wally Barnes, Alex Forbes, Leslie Compton, Joe Mercer (captain), Freddie Cox, Jimmy Logie, Peter Goring, Reg Lewis, Denis Compton.

13 QUOTES FROM ARSÈNE WENGER

"I did not see the incident"................. 1996
"I did not see the incident"................. 1997
"I did not see the incident"................. 1998
"I did not see the incident"................. 1999
"I did not see the incident"................. 2000
"I did not see the incident"................. 2001
"I did not see the incident"................. 2002
"I did not see the incident"................. 2003
"I did not see the incident"................. 2004
"I did not see the incident"................. 2005
"I did not see the incident"................. 2006
"I did not see the incident"................. 2007
"I did not see the incident"................. 2008

THE THINGS THEY SAY – IX

"When my son Ken qualified as a solicitor"
Herbert Chapman reveals his proudest day

THE RIVALS – ARSENAL V MANCHESTER UNITED

In recent years the rivalry between the two clubs – and between Arsène Wenger and Sir Alex Ferguson – has become intense with both sides bidding to outdo each other, not just on the pitch but also in the psychological battle conducted in the newspapers. There was, however, animus before Arsène Wenger's arrival and in 1992 – the season they won the league – Arsenal with George Graham in charge had two points deducted after a 21-player brawl at Old Trafford. The situation between Arsenal and Manchester United has probably worsened since Wenger took over although the intensely competitive Frenchman is not the reason for this. After all, it takes two to tango. The animosity can probably be dated back to 1996-97, Arsène Wenger's first season in charge. It was then that Alex Ferguson moaned that his team's chance of winning the league and the European Cup were hampered by the league fixtures and asked for the season to be lengthened. Wenger hit back saying, "It's wrong for the season to be extended so that Manchester United can rest and win everything." Naturally, Ferguson blew his top and said that Wenger was "a novice and should keep his opinions to Japanese football". In *The Sunday Times* on 3 January 1999, Ferguson criticised Arsenal's disciplinary record claiming, "I'll tell you what they do and I've spoken to other managers about this, and they all agree. When Arsenal are not doing well in a game, they turn it into a battle to try to make the opposition lose concentration. The number of fights involving Arsenal is more than Wimbledon in their heyday." He later claimed that he had written to Wenger to apologise saying he had been "stitched up" – i.e. it was said off the record. Wenger said that "if he sent it, it must have been by horse".

Manchester United 6 Arsenal 1 – 26 April 1952

Arsenal had hopes of doing the double in 1951-52. With seven games remaining, the two teams were on level points. After a postponement due to snow, Arsenal had to play Chelsea twice in the FA Cup Semi Final before progressing to Wembley for the final. The matches depleted the strength of the ageing Arsenal side and they began to falter. A week before the FA Cup Final Arsenal travelled to Old Trafford knowing that to prevent United winning the title Arsenal had to win by seven clear goals. It was not to be and United put six past Arsenal before a crowd

MANCHESTER UNITED'S PAUL INCE AND ARSENAL'S MICHAEL THOMAS

of 53,651. Arsenal: George Swindin, Wally Barnes, Lionel Smith, Alex Forbes, Arthur Shaw, Joe Mercer (captain), Freddie Cox, Peter Goring, Cliff Holton, Reg Lewis, Don Roper.

Arsenal 4 Manchester United 5 – 1 February 1958

The last match played in England by the Busby Babes before their ill-fated journey to Belgrade. The game was played before 63,578 spectators and was thrilling end-to-end stuff. After ten minutes, Duncan Edwards put United one in front, Jack Kelsey not having a chance to block the powerful shot. Bobby Charlton put the northerners two up after half an hour. Tommy Taylor made it 3-0. As with future and past teams, Arsenal refused to surrender and Davy Herd pulled one back before Jimmy Bloomfield scored twice to pull the scores back to three-all. Dennis Viollet headed home to make it 4-3 to United all before half time. Taylor scored in the second half to make it 5-3. Derek Tapscott scored what would be his last goal for Arsenal to make it 4-5 – he moved to Second Division Cardiff City in September of 1958 for £10,000. It ended that way although Vic Groves almost equalised. Tapscott later commented, "I were the last fella to score against the Busby Babes in England. But I wish to God I wasn't." Five days after the match, 23 people of the 44 on board British European Airways Flight 609 destined for Manchester Airport including eight of the United squad (Geoff Bent, Roger Byrne, Eddie Colman, Duncan Edwards {died in hospital 15 days later}, Mark Jones, David Pegg, Tommy Taylor and Billy Whelan) would be dead in the Munich air disaster. Arsenal: Jack Kelsey, Stan Charlton, Evans, Gerry Ward, Jim Fotheringham, Dave Bowen (captain), Vic Groves, Derek Tapscott, David Herd, Jimmy Bloomfield, Gordon Nutt.

Manchester United 0 Arsenal 1 – 20 October 1990

Arsenal went to Old Trafford with an unbeaten record, having won against Wimbledon, Luton Town, Chelsea, Nottingham Forest and Norwich City. Arsenal had much of the play and it was not that surprising when Anders Limpar scored to give the Gunners the lead. Controversially, the United keeper Les Sealey grabbed the ball after it had gone over the line but the referee was close enough to allow the goal. The game before 47,232 fans became rougher and when Nigel Winterburn tackled Denis Irwin, the United players thought that the Arsenal left-back had been unnecessarily tough. Players from both sides squared up to each other while other cool-headed team mates tried to separate the factions. In the end, 21 players became involved (David Seaman was the lone dissenter.) Unsurprisingly, Alex Ferguson got involved. In less than 120 seconds, it was all over but the FA punished both clubs deducting two points from Arsenal and one from United. The Arsenal board were equally unhappy and fined manager George Graham and five players a fortnight's wages. Arsenal: David Seaman, Lee Dixon, Nigel Winterburn, Mickey Thomas, Steve Bould, Tony Adams (captain), David Rocastle (Perry Groves), Paul Davis, Alan Smith, Paul Merson, Anders Limpar.

Manchester United 0 Arsenal 1 – 14 March 1998

Arsenal travelled to Old Trafford knowing that a win would set them on course to win the Premier League title – putting them six points ahead of the Red Devils with three games in hand. Arsenal were put under pressure – as always – in Manchester but the defence held out capped by a great performance by stand-in goalie Alex Manninger replacing the injured David Seaman. Marc Overmars played brilliantly running rings round the United defence and coming close to scoring on several occasions. On 79 minutes, Anelka played Overmars on and the Dutchman put the ball neatly through Peter Schmeichel's legs for the only goal of the game. Arsenal: Alex Manninger, Lee Dixon, Nigel Winterburn, Ray Parlour (Remi Garde), Martin Keown, Tony Adams (captain), Patrick Vieira, Emmanuel Petit, Marc Overmars, Dennis Bergkamp, Christopher Wreh (Nicolas Anelka).

Manchester United 0 Arsenal 1 – 8 May 2002

Having won the FA Cup, Arsenal had the chance to achieve their third double by beating Manchester United at Old Trafford before 67,580 fans. Arsenal had several injury problems and Wenger left out Adams and Henry (both had knee problems) although the striker was on the bench. Kanu replaced Henry up front. At first referee Paul Durkin allowed some leeway, realising what a high-pressure game it was. Finally, United's behaviour became too much and the referee booked Scholes, Neville and Keane all within the first 26 minutes. After one blatant tackle too many Durkin reached for the red card and sentenced Keane to an early bath. With 57 minutes gone, Sylvain Wiltord scored when Barthez was unable to hold a shot from Freddie Ljungberg. The game ended with just one goal between the teams but it was enough to bring the championship to Highbury. Arsenal also became the first team for more than a century to go an entire season unbeaten away from home. Arsène Wenger said, "What this team has achieved is tremendous and will remain in history. This is not only a team of good players, it is one of togetherness." The ever-magnanimous Alex Ferguson said, "They are scrappers who rely on belligerence – we were the better team." Arsenal: David Seaman, Lauren, Ashley Cole, Ray Parlour, Martin Keown, Sol Campbell, Patrick Vieira (captain), Edu, Freddie Ljungberg, Sylvain Wiltord, Nwankwo Kanu (Lee Dixon).

Manchester United 0 Arsenal 2 – 15 February 2003

The fifth round of the FA Cup and holders Arsenal were drawn away to deadly rivals Manchester United. Old Trafford was packed with 67,209 fans waiting the latest battle between the two giants. Wenger rested both Thierry Henry and Dennis Bergkamp. The game began fiercely and three players received a yellow card in the first seven minutes. Paul Scholes and Ruud van Nistelrooy were booked for fouls, while Arsenal captain Patrick Vieira was shown the yellow card for dissent. The referee at one stage even called captains Roy Keane and Vieira together to tell them to calm down their players. Keane (who else?) became the fourth player to be booked when he fouled Robert Pirès. With half an hour to go, Ryan Giggs missed a sitter – with an open goal he punted the ball over the bar. On 35 minutes Edu took a free kick from 25 yards out and saw it whiz past Fabien Barthez thanks to a deflection from David Beckham's shoulder. After 52 minutes, Wiltord made it 2-0 thanks to an assist from Edu. It was the after match activities that received as much coverage as the game itself. Alex Ferguson was so furious at his team's performance that he kicked a boot across the dressing room that hit Beckham in the eye necessitating according to some reports stitches. Publicity hungry Beckham made sure the world saw his injury by wearing an Alice band the next time he was seen in public. Ferguson attempted to play down the incident. "It was a freakish incident. If I tried it 100 or a million times it couldn't happen again. If I could I would have carried on playing!" He did refuse to reveal what really happened. "I have to stress whatever happens in the dressing room remains sacrosanct. There is no way I would betray the trust of the players however much benefit there may be." The excitement did not stop him having his usual moan about the match, though. He said, "Arsenal's players bullied the referee and got away with it." Arsenal:

David Seaman, Lauren, Ashley Cole, Ray Parlour, Martin Keown, Sol Campbell, Edu, Patrick Vieira (captain), Robert Pirès (Giovanni van Bronckhorst), Francis Jeffers (Thierry Henry), Sylvain Wiltord (Kolo Touré).

Manchester United 0 Arsenal 0 – 21 September 2003

The teams met in the league for the first time since the controversial Community Shield on Sunday 10 August 2003, which Manchester United won 4-3 on penalties after the game ended 1-1 in normal time. The man in the middle was Steve Bennett who was also in charge for the Community Shield match. After 21 minutes, Roy Keane became the first of eight players to receive a yellow card. Neither team gave any quarter. On 77 minutes, Patrick Vieira was shown the yellow card for a foul on United's Quinton Fortune. Three minutes later, Vieira was shown a second yellow for what referee Bennet adjudged to be a foul on Ruud van Nistelrooy. Van Nistelrooy was penalised for jumping into Vieira but recoiled as the Arsenal midfielder appeared to kick out from a prone position. It was Arsenal's 52nd sending off since Arsène Wenger took charge. Both sets of players engaged in a shoving match and van Nistelrooy and Jens Lehmann were shown yellow cards in the mêlée. In injury time, United substitute Diego Forlan collapsed after an innocuous challenge from Martin Keown and the referee pointed to the spot. Van Nistelrooy stepped up to take it and for the third successive time missed, smacking the ball against the crossbar. The Arsenal players were jubilant and let the Dutchman know their feelings. The game which attracted 67,639 people, ended goalless and Arsenal returned to the top of the Premier League. Arsenal: Jens Lehmann, Kolo Touré, Ashley Cole, Patrick Vieira (captain), Lauren, Martin Keown, Ray Parlour, Gilberto Silva, Freddie Ljungberg, Dennis Bergkamp (Edu), Thierry Henry.

Three days later, on Wednesday 24 September 2003, six Arsenal and two Manchester United players were charged and one warned by the Football Association for their behaviour at the game. Arsenal were also charged with failing to control their players. The Arsenal players were: Lauren who faced four charges including two of improper conduct for "confronting van Nistelrooy after Vieira's sending-off, and for confronting Giggs after the final whistle"and two counts of violent behaviour for "kicking out at Fortune following the penalty award and for forcibly pushing van Nistelrooy in the back following the final whistle"; Martin Keown received one charge of improper conduct for "confronting van Nistelrooy following the penalty miss" and one charge of violent behaviour "for striking van Nistelrooy on the back of the head following the final whistle"; Ray Parlour faced one charge of improper conduct for "confronting van Nistelrooy after the final whistle" and a further charge of violent behaviour for "grabbing at Gary Neville from behind shortly afterwards"; Ashley Cole faced one charge of improper conduct for "his involvement in a confrontation with Ronaldo after the final whistle"; Jens Lehmann faced one charge of improper conduct for "confronting referee Steve Bennett after Vieira's second yellow card and for then persistently seeking to confront van Nistelrooy"; and Patrick Vieira faced one charge of improper conduct for "failing to leave the field of play following his sending-off, and for instead seeking to confront van Nistelrooy and engaging in a verbal exchange with fourth official Neale Barry". Arsenal were fined £175,000 and given a warning about their future conduct. Lauren received a £40,000 fine and a four match suspension. Keown was suspended for three games and fined £20,000. Vieira was banned for one game and fined £20,000; Parlour also for one match but with a £10,000 fine while Ashley Cole was only fined, albeit £10,000. Arsène Wenger commented, "We should not have reacted like we did. But I find the sensitivity of this country very selective. Suddenly the whole of England is shocked, as if there's never any violence in your society. [The media] have the right to say Arsenal are a dirty team and should have been fined £700,000. But you will never, ever find anyone in my club that I told to go out and kick someone. If you find him, introduce him to me and I will face him. Even if you hang us, that is not enough for some people. They want us hanged twice, and in Hyde Park, in front of the whole country."

Manchester United 2 Arsenal 0 – 24 October 2004

Arsenal arrived at Old Trafford with an unbeaten run of 49 games under their belt looking to extend it to the magic 50. For 73 minutes, the teams played a bad-tempered match with neither side looking likely to break the deadlock. Then Sol Campbell lost Wayne Rooney who he had been brilliantly marking all match. Ryan Giggs passed and Rooney ran, Campbell made an attempt to tackle and Rooney fell over. Referee Mike Riley pointed to the spot despite claims from all the Arsenal team that

Campbell had not touched Rooney. Jens Lehmann tried some kidology to put off Ruud van Nistelrooy but it didn't work and the Dutchman put United one up. The niggling tackes continued with the Neville brothers being especially hard on José Antonio Reyes. In the final minute, Wayne Rooney added a second to end Arsenal's record. In the tunnel afterwards the antics continued and someone hit Alex Ferguson with a slice of pizza. Wenger said that referee Riley had a habit of favouring United and that van Nistelrooy had cheated. The FA charged Wenger with misconduct and fined him £15,000. Arsenal: Jens Lehmann, Lauren, Ashley Cole, Freddie Ljungberg, Sol Campbell, Kolo Touré, Patrick Vieira (captain), Edu, José Antonio Reyes (Robert Pirès), Thierry Henry, Dennis Bergkamp.

Arsenal 2 Manchester United 4 – 1 February 2005

A grudge match even before the opening whistle. Referee Graham Poll remembered that neither team wanted to leave their dressing room first and he asked Arsène Wenger to get his team ready which he agreed to do before making the same request of Alex Ferguson who replied that Roy Keane was not ready. When finally the teams lined up Vieira began a verbal battle with Gary Neville then Keane and Vieira had words. Keane recalled, "Vieira was bragging about all the things he'd done in Senegal. I said to him, 'If you're so fucking worried about Senegal why don't you play for them?'" Poll recalled that he considered sending both men off which he would have been within his rights to do. Footage available on the internet shows Poll trying to calm Keane who is telling the referee that Vieira "had better shut his fucking mouth". When it came to the pre-match toss-up, neither man would shake the other's hand nor would they call heads or tails. In the first two minutes Poll awarded six free kicks as the two teams battled for supremacy. Finally, in the 36th minute Vieira opened the scoring for Arsenal but Ryan Giggs equalised before Dennis Bergkamp put Arsenal back into the lead. Cristiano Ronaldo scored twice in four minutes to put United into the lead and in the 89th minute John O'Shea made it four for United and three points plus two victories over Arsenal in that season. The crowd was 38,164. Refree Poll booked six players – two from Arsenal and four from the Red Devils – as well as sending off a United player. Arsenal: Manuel Almunia, Lauren (Cesc Fàbregas), Ashley Cole, Freddie Ljungberg, Sol Campbell (Justin Hoyte), Pascal Cygan, Mathieu Flamini (José Antonio Reyes), Patrick Vieira (captain), Robert Pirès, Thierry Henry, Dennis Bergkamp.

TRANSFERS THAT FAILED TO PAY OFF

Bryn Jones

In June 1938, Arsenal paid Wolverhampton Wanderers what was then a world record sum for Bryn Jones. On Saturday 27 August, Jones scored on his debut against Portsmouth. He also found the net in two of his next games. However, the goals dried up and he was only to get one more before the end of the season. When Arsenal played Derby County on Wednesday 14 September 1938 at Highbury, the Gunners went down 2-1. A reporter from the *Derby Evening Telegraph* commented, "Arsenal have a big problem. Spending £14,000 on Bryn Jones has not brought the needed thrust into the attack. The little Welsh inside-left is clearly suffering from too much publicity, and is obviously worried. He is a nippy and quite useful inside-left, but his limitations are marked." In his first season at Highbury, Jones hit the net just four times in 30 league appearances and Arsenal finished a disappointing fifth in the First Division. Teammate Cliff Bastin said, "I thought at the time this was a bad transfer, and subsequent events did nothing to alter my views. I had played against Bryn in club and international matches and had ample opportunity to size him up." Another teammate was Bernard Joy, later to become a highly respected sports journalist, said, "Do we write Bryn Jones down as a gamble that failed, or would he have been a success eventually? The outbreak of war in September 1939 prevented us from ever finding the complete answer. There were signs before then that, as James had done, he was weathering the bad patch which always seems to follow a change of style from an attacking to a foraging inside-forward... My own view, however, is that Jones's modesty was the barrier to achieving the key role Arsenal had intended for him. He could not regard the spotlight as a challenge to produce his best; all the time it irked him, making him self-conscious and uneasy." Arsenal manager George Allison claimed that Jones needed time to settle in but Jones would not get that time. A certain Adolf Hitler had other ideas. Jones joined the British Army and served with the Royal Artillery in Italy and North Africa during the Second World War. When the war was over and league football resumed, Bryn Jones was 34-years-old. The following season Jones lost his place to Jimmy Logie. Jones only played in seven games for the team that won the First Division title. On Wednesday 25 May 1949, during a tour of Brazil, Arsenal played Vasco de Gama in Rio de Janeiro. The home side triumphed 1-0 and their excitable supporters invaded the pitch. As the authorities battled to contain the invasion, a Brazilian policeman accidentally hit Jones on the head. So severe were his injuries that on doctor's advice he decided to retire from football. In 137 games for Arsenal at all levels, Bryn Jones had found the net 18 times.

Peter Marinello

On Friday 2 January 1970, Arsenal signed Peter Marinello for £100,000. Good things were expected of the young Scot, but he failed to deliver making just one full appearance during the double-winning season. After just 43 first-team appearances, Marinello was off-loaded to Portsmouth. His last appearance in an Arsenal shirt was as a sub in the FA Cup against Bradford City on Saturday 3 February 1973. One Arsenal director commented when Marinello joined the club: "We've signed the nearest thing in football to The Beatles." It was a shame that it turned out to be Ringo.

Clive Allen

On Thursday 12 June 1980, Terry Neill paid £1.2m to sign Allen from Queens Park Rangers. The move made him Britain's sixth million-pound footballer. After a medical, Allen signed a contract which Neill described as being "for a long time" – the player also received £80,000 as his share of the transfer money. Neill said, "We don't do things lightly here. Our supporters deserve the best and that is what I believe we have given them by buying Clive." Allen stayed at Arsenal long enough to play three pre-season friendlies in the red and white shirt but on Tuesday 12 August 1980 was sold before the start of the 1980-81 season in a deal that saw left-back Kenny Sansom come to Highbury with Allen and reserve goalie Paul Barron go to Loftus Road.

Lee Chapman

On Sunday 1 August 1982, Lee Chapman signed for Arsenal for £500,000 from Stoke City with the fee set by a tribunal. Chapman made his Arsenal debut against his old club on Saturday 28 August 1982 when Arsenal lost 2-1 at the Victoria Ground. Chapman was injured in training and became unhappy at Highbury wanting to leave. On Thursday 1 December 1983, he did leave north London for Sunderland for £100,000 having scored just four goals in 23 League games. However, he played 28 matches for the reserve side in the Football Combination side and hit the back of the net 23 times.

Jimmy Carter

In October 1991, George Graham paid Liverpool £500,000 to sign Jimmy Carter. Carter had signed for the Anfield club for a remarkable £800,000 supposedly as a replacement for John Barnes. On Sunday 8 December 1991, Carter made his Arsenal debut coming on as a substitute against Nottingham Forest as the Gunners lost 3-2. Over the course of the next four years, Carter played just 25 league matches for Arsenal until he was off-loaded with a free transfer in June 1995.

Francis Jeffers

Arsène Wenger paid Everton £8m for Jeffers on 14 June 2001. Jeffers said, "It's a massive club, one of the biggest in Europe and for them to be interested in me is magnificent. Playing with world class players I'm definitely looking to improve." Thierry Henry had said that Arsenal needed "a fox in the box". Unfortunately, this was a box marked return to sender and in 2003, Jeffers was returned to Everton on loan before being sold to Charlton Athletic for £2.6million on 10 August 2004.

Luis Boa Morte

"Blimey, it's me," said Ian Wright of his doppelganger Boa Morte. Unfortunately, he didn't replicate the similarity on the pitch. One of Arsène Wenger's earliest signings (for £1.75million), Boa Morte made his debut as a substitute at Southampton on 23 August 1997. His last appearance for Arsenal was as a second half substitute away to Sunderland on 14 August 1999. He made just 25 first team appearances before he went to Southampton in August 1999 for £500,000.

Davor Šuker

Arsène Wenger was optimistic about Šuker when he signed him from Real Madrid in 1999. Suker had been a regular goal scorer for all his previous clubs Osijek, Dinamo Zagreb and Sevilla and Wenger hoped that the Croat would be able to recreate that form at Highbury. He made his league debut as a substitute on 22 August 1999 in the 2-1 home defeat by Manchester United. Šuker scored twice against Aston Villa in a 3-1 win but he failed to set Highbury alight and moved to West Ham United. Šuker had further failed to endear himself to the Highbury faithful by missing a penalty against Galatasaray in the Uefa Cup Final.

SCREWED

Two Arsenal players who became prison warders after hanging up their boots were Ian McKechnie and Ian Ure, who was a warder at the infamous Low Moss Prison in Glasgow.

THE ARSENAL – DECADE BY DECADE: 1910s

1910-11

First Division	P	W	D	L	F	A	W	D	L	F	A	Pts
10. Arsenal	38	9	6	4	24	14	4	6	9	17	35	38

FA Cup: Second round

1911-12

First Division	P	W	D	L	F	A	W	D	L	F	A	Pts
10. Arsenal	38	12	3	4	38	19	3	5	11	17	40	38

FA Cup: First round

1912-13

First Division	P	W	D	L	F	A	W	D	L	F	A	Pts
20. Arsenal	38	1	8	10	11	31	2	4	13	15	43	18

FA Cup: Second round

1913-14

Second Division	P	W	D	L	F	A	W	D	L	F	A	Pts
3. Arsenal	38	14	3	2	34	10	6	6	7	20	28	49

FA Cup: First round

1914-15

Second Division	P	W	D	L	F	A	W	D	L	F	A	Pts
5. Arsenal	38	15	1	3	52	13	4	4	11	17	28	43

FA Cup: Second round

1915-1919 the Football League was suspended due to the First World War.

1919-20

First Division	P	W	D	L	F	A	W	D	L	F	A	Pts
10. Arsenal	42	11	5	5	32	21	4	7	10	24	37	42

FA Cup: Second round

THE RIVALS – ARSENAL V TOTTENHAM HOTSPUR

Until recent years, the bitterest rivalry has been reserved for Arsenal's neighbours at the wrong end of the Seven Sisters Road. Despite the wars of words between Arsène Wenger and Sir Alex Ferguson, Arsenal fans still reserve a genuine loathing for Spurs and the feeling is reciprocated. The first match between the two teams occurred on Saturday 19 November 1887 and ended a quarter of an hour early because of poor light with Spurs leading 2-1. The first league match between the clubs was in the First Division, on 4 December 1909 and Woolwich Arsenal won 1-0. Four years later, in 1913, Arsenal were relegated to the Second Division for the only time in their history after their worst ever season (then the worst ever record for any First Division club – P38 W3 D12 L23). During the First World War Arsenal chairman Sir Henry Norris won acclaim as a member of the committee that raised the footballers' battalion of the Middlesex regiment, and he personally raised three brigades of artillery from the Fulham area, where he was recruiting officer with the rank of colonel. In December 1918, he was elected Tory MP for Fulham East, a seat he held for four years. In 1919, the Football League resumed and John McKenna of the FA management committee suggested that the First Division be expanded from 20 to 22 clubs. Arsenal seemed to have no chance of joining the elite having finished fifth in the Second Division behind Derby County, Preston North End, Barnsley and Wolverhampton Wanderers and head of Birmingham City on goal average. Arsenal's goal average was 1.683 while Birmingham's was 1.590. Chelsea and Spurs finished bottom of the First Division and it was widely expected that both clubs would gain a reprieve and be allowed to stay in the top flight. However, Spurs reckoned without the wily Sir Henry Norris. He secretly canvassed every committee member (except Spurs) and suggested that Arsenal were deserving of promotion. He also said that because Arsenal were based in London, directors of other clubs visiting Highbury could take their wives to the West End which would be so much better than dinner in Birmingham or Wolverhampton. Norris met the chairman of Chelsea and told him that his club was safe and would be in the First Division. Norris said that Arsenal deserved promotion because of "their long service to league football", ignoring the fact that Wolves had been members for longer. When the vote was taken, Arsenal received 18,

TONY ADAMS HEADS THE WINNER IN THE 1993 FA CUP SEMI FINAL AGAINST SPURS

Spurs just eight, Barnsley five, Wolves four, Nottingham Forest three, Birmingham two and Hull City only one. Arsenal were back in the First Division where they have been ever since and Spurs languished in the Second Division. The rivalry, which had begun six years earlier when Arsenal invaded Tottenham's hinterland, was cemented. The first derby match after Arsenal's 1913 move to north London was a First Division match on 15 January 1921 at White Hart Lane. Spurs won 2-1. Here are some remarkable games between the two teams.

Tottenham Hotspur 1 Arsenal 2 – 23 September 1922

A match so ill-tempered that an FA Commission of Inquiry was summoned to investigate and Spurs were warned that White Hart Lane would be closed if there was a repeat of the crowd violence. In a masterly understatement *The Times* man reported, "It was a not a satisfactory game from any point of view." Within ten minutes a Spurs player was accidentally injured as he ran and then a second player and a third was injured in a clash with Arthur Hutchins. For five minutes in the first half Spurs were down to nine men. Within five minutes of the restart Reg Boreham scored for Arsenal putting the ball in the right-hand corner of the net. It was after Arsenal went ahead that the home fans turned nasty "and militated against their own side". On 80 minutes, Boreham added a second but Spurs pulled one back in the last minute the Arsenal players having stopped because – irony – they thought the Spurs forwards offside. The match was watched by 40,582 fans and left Arsenal in 15th place in the first division, five places below Spurs. Arsenal: Steven Dunn, Frank Bradshaw, Arthur Hutchins, Alf Baker, Clem Voysey, Alex Graham, Jock Rutherford, Harry White, Andy Young, Reg Boreham, Billy Blyth.

Arsenal 5 Tottenham Hotspur 1 – 20 October 1934

The biggest home win over Spurs. *The Times* reporter said that Arsenal were expected to win and duly beat Spurs and the 5-1 margin was no more than the Gunners deserved. The match as with nearly all north London derbies was played at a quick pace with players rushing hither and thither not concentrating on utilising their skills. Arsenal, *The Times* man concluded, had no weak spots and played as a team while Spurs played as individuals. The crowd of 70,544 watched a superlative performance by Arsenal and Pat Beasley opened the scoring on the half hour. Ten minutes later, T Evans of Spurs tried to clear a Drake attack and succeeded only in putting the ball into the top left hand corner of his own goal. Drake scored his first and Arsenal's third a minute later and the teams went in for their half-time oranges with the Gunners three to the good. On 50 minutes, Drake made it 4-0 before scoring his hat-trick. *The Times* man said that if both teams had taken all their chances Arsenal could have won 12-3 – now that would have been a game! Arsenal: Frank Moss, George Male, Eddie Hapgood (captain), Jack Crayston, Herbie Roberts, Bob John, Pat Beasley, Ray Bowden, Ted Drake, Alex James, Cliff Bastin.

Tottenham Hotspur 0 Arsenal 6 – 6 March 1935

The match – Arsenal's biggest away win over Spurs – left Arsenal at the top of the league and Spurs looking likely to be relegated. The game was not so much a match as a massacre and it was only the woodwork and the Spurs goalie that stopped the goals for Arsenal being in double figures. Alf Kirchen scored two goals on his debut for the Gunners who were without Herbie Roberts, Alex James and Eddie Hapgood. Ted Drake opened Arsenal's account after six minutes and Peter Dougall scored a third before half-time. In the second half Drake scored his second and Cliff Bastin hit the sixth from the penalty spot. The Arsenal element of the 47,714 crowd went home happy. Arsenal: Frank Moss, George Male, Leslie Compton, Jack Crayston, Norman Sidey, Wilf Copping, Alf Kirchen, Rob Davidson, Ted Drake, Peter Dougall, Cliff Bastin.

Tottenham Hotspur 0 Arsenal 1 – 3 May 1971

The last match of the 1970-71 season and Arsenal needed to either win or get a goalless draw or the championship title would go to Leeds United. Spurs needed three points to qualify for Europe but they still had a game to play (against Arsenal's semi-final rivals Stoke City) so a draw would have been okay for them. (In those days, it was two points for a win. Three points was introduced in 1981.) Spurs manager Bill Nicholson said, "We are tremendously proud of our double achievement. I suppose some other club has got to do it again sometime, but we will be doing our best to make sure it isn't Arsenal." Spurs also offered their players a win bonus of £400. The desire to see the match was immense and it was estimated that almost 100,000 people were locked out when the game began – 51,992 made it into White Hart Lane. The Monday night match was tight end-to-end stuff. Captain McLintock bellowed out orders and encouragement "But I might as well have been talking to myself. You just couldn't hear a thing out there." Both goalies – Bob Wilson and Pat Jennings – made great saves to keep their sides in the match. Manager Mee sat in the stand at White Hart Lane alongside chairman Denis Hill-Wood and allowed Don Howe to run things tactically from the bench. Then with three minutes to go, John Radford forced a typically brilliant save from Pat Jennings, so brilliant in fact that the Spurs defence seemed to stop to admire it. George Armstrong did not stand around and clipped the rebound across the goal for Ray Kennedy to head Arsenal in to the lead. Kennedy was to later comment that he was not sure if he had wished that he hadn't scored because it added extra pressure to the game. Arsenal packed their own goal area but even then Bob Wilson in typically heroic fashion had to fling himself at the feet of the opposition and his own team to grab the ball. Finally, referee Kevin Howley, officiating in his last game, blew his whistle and the league trophy was on its way to Arsenal Stadium. The Arsenal fans invaded the pitch and Don Howe was worried that some of the team might be injured in the jubilation. "But thank goodness," he said, "no one was injured and all that went missing was a few shirts." In a magnanimous gesture, Bill Nicholson took champagne to the Arsenal dressing room. The Arsenal team repaired to the White Hart pub in Southgate for a private party where they drank until the early hours. Arsenal: Bob Wilson, Pat Rice, Bob McNab, Eddie Kelly, Frank McLintock (captain), Peter Simpson, George Armstrong, George Graham, John Radford, Ray Kennedy, Charlie George.

Tottenham Hotspur 0 Arsenal 5 – 23 December 1978

One of the great performances by an Arsenal side at White Hart Lane with a hat-trick from Alan Sunderland and a world class game from Liam Brady. It was Spurs's first season in the top flight after gaining promotion and they were determined to show that they deserved their place among the big boys. In the midfield, Brady battled for supremacy with Argentinian import Osvaldo Ardiles – and won, convincingly. With just one minute gone, the appropriately named John Pratt bungled a clearance hitting the ball against David Price for Alan Sunderland to pop up and hit the ball past Mark Kendall in the Spurs goal. Pat Jennings returned to White Hart Lane for the first time since his move to Highbury in August 1977 but the Spurs forwards did not trouble him. On 38 minutes, Sunderland scored his second. In the second half, Price missed a sitter and Sunderland hit the bar but the third goal arrived in the 62nd minute courtesy of Frank Stapleton's head. Liam Brady showed his world class with Arsenal's fourth leaving Kendall helpless with a shot to the top corner. Alan Sunderland scored his first hat-trick for the club as Arsenal hit five to end a perfect day – for Gunners fans among the 42,273 crowd at least. Arsenal: Pat Jennings, Pat Rice (captain), Steve Walford, David Price, David O'Leary, Willie Young, Liam Brady, Alan Sunderland, Frank Stapleton, Steve Gatting, Graham Rix.

Tottenham Hotspur 1 Arsenal 2 – 4 March 1987

After two League Cup semi-Final matches ended 2-2 on aggregate, this was the third game and was played at White Hart Lane before 41,005 fans, three days after Arsenal had beaten Spurs 2-1 again at White Hart Lane. For that tie away goals did not count double so the two teams were forced to meet again to settle the contest. For the third successive time ex-Gunner Clive Allen put Spurs ahead. It looked as if Spurs were on their way to Wem-ber-ley and things were not helped when Charlie Nicholas was carried off injured. However, the chaps from White Hart Lane did not anticipate Arsenal's never say die attitude and with just eight minutes to go substitute Ian Allinson levelled the scores. At 9.44pm in injury time David "Rocky" Rocastle popped up to slide the ball under Ray Clemence in the Spurs goal and break Tottenham hearts. Arsenal: John Lukic, Viv Anderson, Kenny Sansom, Michael Thomas, David O'Leary, Tony Adams, David Rocastle, Paul Davis, Niall Quinn, Charlie Nicholas (Ian Allinson), Martin Hayes.

Tottenham Hotspur 3 Arsenal 1 – 14 April 1991

The two teams met for the first time in the FA Cup Semi-Final with Arsenal attempting a second double. Troubled genius Paul Gascoigne scored from a free kick 30 yards out after just five minutes to put Spurs ahead. Gary Lineker put the Lillywhites two-up but Alan Smith scored for Arsenal to make it 2-1 at half time with everything to play for. It was not to be Arsenal's game and Lineker added a third to seal the game for Spurs. Arsenal: David Seaman, Lee Dixon, Nigel Winterburn, Michael

Thomas, Steve Bould, Tony Adams, (captain) Kevin Campbell, Paul Davis, Alan Smith, Paul Merson, Anders Limpar (Perry Groves).

Arsenal 1 Tottenham Hotspur 0 – 4 April 1993

Two years later, and another FA Cup Semi-Final saw Arsenal out for revenge. The game looked as it was heading for a 0-0 stalemate when Arsenal won a free kick in the 79th minute. Paul Merson flicked a ball into the Spurs area and Tony Adams popped up with a header to score the only goal of the game. Arsenal's celebrations were somewhat muted by Lee Dixon's sending off but were on their way to becoming the first team ever to win both domestic cups. Arsenal: David Seaman, Lee Dixon, Nigel Winterburn, David Hillier, Andy Linighan, Tony Adams (captain), Ray Parlour (Alan Smith), Ian Wright, Kevin Campbell (Steve Morrow), Paul Merson, Ian Selley.

Arsenal 3 Tottenham Hotspur 1 – 24 November 1996

A month after Arsène Wenger took over, Arsenal faced Spurs in the first north London derby of the season. Ian Wright put Arsenal ahead with a penalty after Dennis Bergkamp was fouled. Patrick Vieira went down injured and goalie John Lukic threw the ball out so his team mate could get medical attention. Spurs did not keep to the unwritten agreement to return the ball after an injury and scored virtually from the throw-in helped by an unfortunate bounce that saw Lukic score an own goal. As the game neared its end and the rain beat down on Highbury it looked as if the teams would share the points. With ten minutes to go, John Hartson came on to replace David Platt and seemed to energise the Arsenal side. In the 88th minute, Tony Adams volleyed a left footed shot into the Spurs net. A minute or so later, Dennis Bergkamp made it 3-1, slotting past Ian Walker in the Spurs goal. Arsenal: John Lukic, Lee Dixon, Nigel Winterburn, David Platt (John Hartson), Martin Keown, Tony Adams (captain), Steve Bould, Patrick Vieira, Paul Merson, Dennis Bergkamp (Ray Parlour), Ian Wright.

Tottenham Hotspur 4 Arsenal 5 – 13 November 2004

Arsenal-Spurs games are always high-octane affairs with neither side wanting to lose and neither side concerned about the reputation of the other and league performances count for nothing. So it was with this game: on 37 minutes defender Noureddine Naybet put Spurs ahead.

Eight minutes later, Thierry Henry equalised for Arsenal. One-all at half-time but neither fans nor players could expect the goal glut that would define the second half. On 55 minutes, Lauren converted a penalty after Noé Paramot fouled Freddie Ljungberg. After an hour Patrick Vieira made it 3-1 to the Arsenal and the game seemed over. Jermain Defoe scored to make it 3-2 and the game was once more open. Cesc Fàbregas in his first north London derby combined with Thierry Henry to give Ljungberg the chance to make it 4-2. Ledley King made it 4-3 before Robert Pirès made it 5-3 and victory for Arsenal. Then Arsenal relaxed and Frederic Kanoute pulled one back for Spurs with two minutes to go. Nine goals, nine different scorers – three points to Arsenal. Arsenal: Jens Lehmann, Lauren, Ashley Cole, Freddie Ljungberg, Kolo Toure, Pascal Cygan, Patrick Vieira, Cesc Fàbregas, Thierry Henry, Dennis Bergkamp (Robin van Persie), José Antonio Reyes (Robert Pirès).

Tottenham Hotspur 5 Arsenal 1 – 22 January 2008

Thanks to Arsène Wenger's decision to give young and untested players (most of who never seem to make first team regulars) experience, Arsenal went down to their first defeat against the old enemy since November 1999 – eight years and 76 days – and the largest losing margin for 25 years. The second semi-final of the League Cup – the one competition Wenger seems not to care if the club win or not – and Arsenal's only realistic hope of silverware in 2007-08 was held at White Hart Lane after a 1-1 draw at the Emirates Stadium. By half time, 35,979 fans had seen Spurs go two to the good thanks to Jermaine Jenas on three minutes and an own goal from Nicklas Bendtner after 27 minutes. In the second half, Spurs were 4-0 up before substitute Emmanuel Adebayor pulled one back in the 70th minute but Steed Malbranque scored a fifth goal in injury time to put Spurs through to the League Cup Final 6-2 on aggregate. It was the first time that Arsenal lost after Emmanuel Adebayor scored and the first time Spurs had beaten an Arsène Wenger Arsenal side. The *Daily Mail* reported, "Arsenal were hamstrung by Arsène Wenger's decision to start with a predominantly second-string side." (To add insult to injury Spurs went on to win the competition beating Chelsea 2-1 at Wembley on 24 February 2008.) Arsenal: Łukasz Fabiański, Bacary Sagna, Armand Traoré (Eduardo), Alexander Hleb, William Gallas (captain), Justin Hoyte, Denílson (Cesc Fàbregas), Nicklas Bendtner, Theo Walcott (Emmanuel Adebayor), Gilberto, Abou Diaby.

UP FOR THE CUP – VI

Arsenal 0 Newcastle United 1

It was a wait of only two years for the next FA Cup Final appearance on Saturday 3 May 1952 against the Geordies of Newcastle United before another Wembley full house of 100,000. Arsenal this time were on the other side of the famous result as Newcastle won 1-0. The Arsenal team was beset with injuries both before and during the game. Ray Daniel played with a broken wrist, Doug Lishman had a septic wound and Jimmy Logie had internal bleeding from a leg wound. In the early stages of the game, Wally Barnes injured himself after 35 minutes and had to go off for treatment. He hobbled back on but the pain was too much and Arsenal were reduced to ten men for the rest of the final. With six minutes to go, Holton and Roper were injured but referee Arthur Ellis (later to be an adjudicator on *It's A Knockout*) waved play on and Bobby Mitchell crossed for George Robledo to head home Newcastle's winner. Arsenal: George Swindin, Wally Barnes, Lionel Smith, Alex Forbes, Ray Daniel, Joe Mercer (captain), Freddie Cox, Jimmy Logie, Cliff Holton, Doug Lishman, Don Roper.

FOOTBALL'S COMING HOME

Until recently the backroom boys of a football club have been a small group usually including manager, coach, trainer and one or two others. In modern times, the backroom staffs can be huge. The following – all ex-Arsenal players – are now involved behind the scenes at the Emirates.

Steve Bould .... Head coach of under-18 academy side
Liam Brady.. Head of youth development
Paul Davis.. Youth team coach
Steve Gatting... Youth team coach
David Court .... Assistant head of youth development
Charlie George.....................................Arsenal Legends tour guide
Gilles Grimandi .... Scout
Sammy Nelson ....Arsenal Legends tour guide
John Radford.......................................Arsenal Legends tour guide
Pat Rice ....Assistant manager
Kenny Sansom......................................Arsenal Legends tour guide

THEY ALSO SERVED...

Bob Wilson, Jimmy Rimmer, Pat Jennings, John Lukic, and David Seaman were five giants between the sticks at Arsenal from 1969 until 2003. In that period, other keepers joined the club hoping to unseat the famous five but all failed. Here I salute those who also served…

Malcolm Webster

England youth goalie Webster became an apprentice with Arsenal in May 1966, turning professional in January 1968. He had a brief three-match run between the sticks in 1969 after Bob Wilson was injured. He made his debut for Arsenal in the home derby against Spurs on Tuesday 16 September 1969, which the Gunners lost 3-2. He was beaten twice in the next game against Manchester United, also at Highbury, which ended in a 2-2 draw. On Saturday 27 September, Arsenal travelled to Stamford Bridge where they lost 3-0. Manager Bertie Mee felt that 18-year-old Webster did not have the experience to be Arsenal's first choice goalie and he signed Geoff Barnett. Webster also appeared for the Gunners in two League Cup ties and one Uefa Cup match although he never appeared in a winning team. Webster played more than 150 representative games for Arsenal before he joined Fulham in December 1969. He later moved to Southend United and Cambridge United for whom he played more than 500 first team games. It is likely that if Wilson had not been injured Webster would have matured in the reserves and may have come into his own in the mid-Seventies as Arsenal's goalie.

Geoff Barnett

One of English football's unluckiest players, curly-headed Barnett joined Everton in 1962 and looked set for a promising career, winning schoolboy and under-21 honours with England while at Goodison Park but found himself kept out of the Toffeemen's goal by the form of Gordon West and Andy Rankin. In 1969 – after seven years on Merseyside and just ten league appearances – he joined Arsenal for £35,000 after Bob Wilson broke his arm nine games into the season. Barnett made his debut against Coventry City on Saturday 4 October 1969 and Arsenal lost 1-0. During that season, Barnett made 11 league appearances and kept a clean sheet in the second round of the Fairs Cup against Sporting Lisbon (including saving a penalty in the first leg) but as soon as Wilson recovered, Barnett found himself in the reserves. Wilson was ever present during the double-winning season but Barnett got his chance the following season when Wilson was injured again and gave a creditable performance in the 1972 FA Cup Final. Barnett started the 1972-73 season playing 25 matches between the sticks as Bob Wilson recovered from injury but as soon as Wilson was fit Barnett was again back in the reserves. In February 1974, Arsenal signed Jimmy Rimmer for £40,000 from Manchester United and it became apparent that despite his loyalty and more than competent service Barnett was never destined to be Arsenal's number one goalkeeper. He played his 49th and last game for the Gunners against Stoke City on Saturday 13 December 1975. The following month he left Highbury for good to join Minnesota Kicks in the North American football league. His only honours for the club were an FA Cup runners-up medal and a Football Combination Cup winners' medal (1969-1970).

Rhys Wilmot

Like Geoff Barnett, Rhys Wilmot showed great loyalty to Arsenal. He signed schoolboy forms for the club in 1977 and turned professional three years later on Friday 8 February 1980 although he did not make his first team debut until Good Friday 28 March 1986 (against Aston Villa – Arsenal won 4-1 at Villa Park). He understudied Pat Jennings, George Wood and then John Lukic, spending time on loan to Hereford United (March 1983) and Leyton Orient (May 198-.). During the 1986-87, he deputised for Lukic six times before losing his place and going on loan to Swansea City on Friday 26 August 1988. On Thursday 23 February 1989, he left Highbury for Plymouth Argyle for a fee of £100,000 after playing 340 representative games for Arsenal.

Paul Barron

Tall and blond, Barron joined Arsenal from Plymouth Argyle in July 1978 for £70,000 as reserve to Pat Jennings, and made his debut on Wednesday 2 August 1978 against Manchester City. A capable keeper, Barron was unable to displace Jennings from between the sticks and played just eight games in two seasons. In 1980, he joined Crystal Palace along with Clive Allen in the deal that brought Kenny Sansom to Highbury. He is currently goalkeeping coach at Newcastle United. Paul Barron was one of two keepers that goalkeeping coach Bob Wilson said that he was most disappointed that they did not achieve as much as they could.

George Wood

In August 1980, Terry Neill paid Everton £140,000 for the services of George Wood, then 28, seeing him as the long-term replacement for 35-year-old Pat Jennings. The Irishman had other ideas and although Wood made 60 appearances for Arsenal over the next three years, Jennings never allowed him an easy ride. In May 1983, Wood was given a free transfer and joined Crystal Palace.

Alan Miller

Epping-born Miller became an apprentice at Arsenal in July 1984 and four years later signed professional terms. He won an FA Youth Cup winner's medal and four England under-21 caps, but found it impossible to unseat John Lukic and David Seaman and went on loan to Plymouth Argyle (November 1988), Birmingham City (December 1991) and West Bromwich Albion (February 1997). His Arsenal debut finally came on Saturday 21 November 1992 in unusual circumstances. He became the first-ever Arsenal keeper to come on as a sub and made seven further appearances over the next two seasons. The change in the substitute rules allowed him to collect some silverware; he picked up an FA Cup, and League Cup winners' medals in 1992-93 and a Uefa Cup Winners' Cup medal in 1993-94 although he was on the bench in all three games. On Friday 12 August 1994, ten years after he joined Arsenal, Miller joined Middlesbrough for £500,000. He later dated *Brookside* actress and reality TV star Claire Sweeney. He retired aged 33 because of a back injury.

Lee Harper

Harper began his career at non-league Sittingbourne before joining Arsenal for £150,000 in June 1994. On Saturday 15 March 1997, he made his one and only appearance for the first team in a 2-0 win over Southampton in the Premier League. In July 1997, he left for Queens Park Rangers who paid £125,000 for his services.

Vince Bartram

On Wednesday 10 August 1994, George Graham paid Bournemouth 40,000 for the services of Bartram. David Seaman's form limited Bartram's appearances to just 12. On Friday 20 March 1998, he signed for Gillingham where he stayed for almost six years. In 2006, he played for Arsenal's Over-35s team.

Alex Manninger

On Tuesday 3 June 1997, Manninger joined Arsenal from Casino Graz as the reserve keeper to David Seaman. That season Seaman was injured and Manninger had an extended run in the team including keeping a clean sheet on six consecutive occasions – a joint club record (see page 131). As was the fate of many keepers when Seaman returned to fitness, Manninger returned to the reserves. He dropped to third choice when Arsène Wenger bought Richard Wright and even went out on loan to Fiorentina for a year. On Thursday 4 July 2002, Manninger signed for RCD Espanyol for £960,000. Manninger was one of two keepers that goalkeeping coach Bob Wilson said that he was most disappointed that they did not achieve as much as they could.

Stuart Taylor

Born in Romford, Essex Stuart Taylor joined Arsenal on Friday 1 August 1997 and to gain experience was loaned to Bristol Rovers (September 1999), Crystal Palace (August 2000), Peterborough United (February 2001) and Leicester City (November 2004). Taylor was widely expected to replace David Seaman and saw off competition from Alex Manninger and Richard Wright for the position between the sticks. In eight years at Highbury, he only played 30 times and when Arsène Wenger signed Jens Lehmann and Manuel Almunia, Taylor saw that the writing was on the wall and, on Monday 27 June 2005, he signed for Aston Villa.

Graham Stack

Stack joined Arsenal on Tuesday 1 August 2000 but suffered injuries and was loaned to Koninklijke Sportkring Beveren. It was not a happy experience – in December 2001, he was attacked when fans ran onto the pitch. He was punched in the face before police restored order. Back at Highbury, he made his first team debut thanks to Arsène Wenger's policy of playing youngsters in League Cup matches, a competition in which he has no apparent interest. On Tuesday 28 October 2003, Stack played against Rotherham United, a game that Arsenal won 9-8 on penalties. He kept his position for the rest of the cup run. On Friday 9 July 2004, he was loaned to Millwall for the 2004-05 season and on Thursday 7 July 2005 went on loan to Reading. In September 2004 – while at Millwall – a 22-year-old

female law student accused Stack, then 23, of sexual assault. However, on Friday 30 September 2005, a jury cleared Stack of the charge and on Sunday 8 January 2006, he signed full-time for Reading.

Richard Wright

Ipswich-born Wright began his career with his home team and gained a reputation for himself that persuaded Arsène Wenger to splash out £6million and a five-year contract on Thursday 5 July 2001 to bring him to Highbury where he would face competition from David Seaman and Alex Manninger for the number one jersey. On Saturday 29 September 2001, 23-year-old Wright made his first-team debut against Derby County but despite an injury to Seaman, he never made the position his own. During a 4-2 defeat by Charlton Athletic, Wright managed to punch the ball into his own net and then injured himself in a Champions League match against Deportivo La Coruna. Recovered, he found himself as third choice keeper behind Seaman and Stuart Taylor. Just a year after he arrived, Wright joined Everton for £3,500,000 on Wednesday 24 July 2002. Richard Wright, Wright, Wright? No, Richard Wrong, Wrong, Wrong.

Rami Shaaban

Stockholm-born Shaaban signed for Arsenal on Friday 30 August 2002 from Djurgårdens IF and made his debut on Tuesday 12 November of that year in the Champions League against PSV Eindhoven in a goalless draw. Twenty-five days later, he played his last game for the Gunners, against Manchester United in the Premier League in a match that Arsenal lost 2-0. On Saturday 17 January 2004, Shaaban went on loan to West Ham United for a month but did not make any first team appearances. On Saturday 19 February 2005, he joined for Brighton & Hove Albion on a short-term deal, before returning to Djurgårdens IF.

The following, also on Arsenal's books as goalkeepers in that period, did not manage to break into the first team: Glenn Johnson (August 1968-1970), Graham Horn (1969-February 1973), Neil Freeman (June 1972-March 1974), Brian Parker (1975-1977), Nick Sullivan (1976-1980), Gary Lewin (1980-1982), Nick Hammond (1985-1987), Andrew Marriott (October 1988-June 1989) and Jim Will (July 1989-June 1994).

FOOD FOR THOUGHT

Modern footballers are aware of the necessity of a good diet – it can prolong careers. In the 1930s, Arsenal – the Bank of England Club – ensured that players travelled in style. Under Herbert Chapman, the players travelled to away games in a private railway carriage and were served champagne and smoked salmon. On the way back they ate fish and chips and drank brown ale. Forty years on, the situation hadn't changed. Alan Ball commented shortly after his transfer from Everton: "They really make their players feel important. When they travel to away matches, they do it in style. It's the best of everything. The coach they travelled in had just about everything. There was waiter service and three-course meals. Anything you wanted was available: smoked salmon, beef salads, every drink you could think of and cigars – even After Eight mints. It was luxury all the way down the line and on foreign trips it was champagne service on the flight and only the best hotels." Another thirty years has passed and under Arsène Wenger things are very different, with a strict players' diet. On one occasion on the coach home the players at the back began a chorus of "We want our chocolate back" after Wenger accused them of eating too much. Freddie Ljungberg recalls the first time he stayed in the team hotel. The players ate at 7pm and then Wenger told them not to eat again. Ljungberg said, "By 10pm I was starving so I ordered spaghetti Bolognese and the next morning I got a terrible bollocking from the boss. I was shocked. He checks all your bills."

UP FOR THE CUP – VII

Arsenal 0 Leeds United 1

On Saturday 2 March 1968, Arsenal played Leeds United before 97,887 spectators in their first League Cup Final. The match ended 1-0 to the Yorkshire side. Ian Ure remembered, "It was not a pleasant game. You wouldn't believe the amount of shirt-pulling, sly kicks and time wasting which Jack Charlton, Johnny Giles and Norman Hunter were doing." Bobby Gould said, "Jack Charlton used to volley you up in the air and Norman Hunter used to thwack you on the way down." In the second half, all 22 players became embroiled in a brawl after Charlton fouled Jim Furnell in the Arsenal goal. Arsenal: Jim Furnell, Peter Storey, Bob McNab, Frank McLintock (captain), Ian Ure, Peter Simpson, John Radford, David Jenkins (Terry Neill), George Graham, Jon Sammels, George Armstrong.

THE THINGS THEY SAY – IX

"We used to have romantic nights in watching films – with his agent. We only ever went out to Tesco. It was embarrassing – I'd get dressed up for a lovely night out and end up at the seafood counter."
    Beth Moutrey, sometime girlfriend of Nicolas Anelka, 2003

THE ARSENAL – DECADE BY DECADE: 1920s

1920-21

First Division	P	W	D	L	F	A	W	D	L	F	A	Pts
9. Arsenal	42	9	8	4	31	25	6	6	9	28	38	44

FA Cup: First round

1921-22

First Division	P	W	D	L	F	A	W	D	L	F	A	Pts
17. Arsenal	42	10	6	5	27	19	5	1	15	20	37	37

FA Cup: Fourth round

1922-23

First Division	P	W	D	L	F	A	W	D	L	F	A	Pts
11. Arsenal	42	13	4	4	38	16	3	6	12	23	46	42

FA Cup: First round

1923-24

First Division	P	W	D	L	F	A	W	D	L	F	A	Pts
19. Arsenal	42	8	5	8	25	24	4	4	13	15	39	33

FA Cup: Second round

1924-25

First Division	P	W	D	L	F	A	W	D	L	F	A	Pts
20. Arsenal	42	12	3	6	33	17	2	2	17	13	41	33

FA Cup: First round

1925-26

First Division	P	W	D	L	F	A	W	D	L	F	A	Pts
2. Arsenal	42	16	2	3	57	19	6	6	9	30	44	52

FA Cup: Sixth round

1926-27

First Division	P	W	D	L	F	A	W	D	L	F	A	Pts
11. Arsenal	42	12	5	4	47	30	5	4	12	30	56	43

FA Cup: Runners-up

1927-28

First Division	P	W	D	L	F	A	W	D	L	F	A	Pts
10. Arsenal	42	10	6	5	49	33	3	9	9	33	53	41

FA Cup: Semi-final

1928-29

First Division	P	W	D	L	F	A	W	D	L	F	A	Pts
9. Arsenal	42	11	6	4	43	25	5	7	9	34	47	45

FA Cup: Sixth round

1929-30

First Division	P	W	D	L	F	A	W	D	L	F	A	Pts
14. Arsenal	42	10	2	9	49	26	4	9	8	29	40	39

FA Cup: Winners

DRAKE SCORES AGAINST ALMOST EVERYONE

George Allison signed Ted Drake, a gas inspector by trade, in March 1934 from Southampton for a fee of £6,000. In his first full season at Highbury (1934-35), Drake scored 42 in 41 appearances including four four-goal hauls – against Birmingham City, Chelsea, Wolves and Middlesbrough – and three hat-tricks. It was a game at Aston Villa on 14 December 1935, in front of a crowd of 70,000, that sealed Drake's fate as an Arsenal legend. Drake began the game carrying an injury, his knee was heavily strapped and then he fell on the perimeter track and cut his arm. Villa took the initiative for the first 15 minutes but by half-time Arsenal were three up thanks to Drake's hat-trick. With an hour played, it was 6-0 and Drake got the lot. The final score 7-1 with all seven scored by Drake. That day he had nine shots on target – seven went in, one was saved by Villa keeper Harry Morton and another hit the post, although according to Drake the ball was over the line. Twelve days later, Bunny Bell of Tranmere Rovers beat Drake's total with nine against Oldham Athletic in the Third Division North, Drake remains the highest individual scorer for the top division.

GUNNERS WHO BECAME GENERALS

1. Tony Adams

The Arsenal legend had a brief (November 2003-November 2004) spell in charge of Wycombe Wanderers who were relegated at the end of the 2003-04 season. Adams commented, "[When I took the job I had to] set aside everything I learned from Arsène Wenger. It's a complete waste of time [in the Second Division]. They just can't take a lot of information on board." On Wednesday 28 June 2006, Adams found a berth as assistant manager of Portsmouth.

2. Colin Addison

The forward had more success as a manager than as a player at Highbury where he played fewer than 30 league games. He managed Newport County, Derby County, Newport County (again), Celta Vigo (in Spain), Hereford United (he was in charge during their 1972 FA Cup giant killing spree), Cadiz CF, Merthyr Tydfil, Deportivo, Merthyr Town, Scarborough, Yeovil Town, Swansea City, Forest Green Rovers and Barry Town.

3. Ian Allinson

After retiring from football, Allinson became manager of Baldock Town and Stotfold Town.

4. Joe Baker

The centre-forward became manager-coach of Scottish junior side Fauldhouse United in 1980.

5. Alan Ball, MBE

The red-headed midfielder became player-manager of Blackpool in February 1980 and had two spells managing Portsmouth (May 1984-January 1989 and February 1998-9 December 1999). He was also boss at Stoke City (sacked in February 1991), Exeter City, Southampton (January 1994-July 1995) and Manchester City (July 1996-1996). At Southampton goalie Dave Beasant said, "Alan Ball and I didn't see eye to eye, and that had nothing to do with his being 5ft 3in and me being 6ft 4in." Ball died of a heart attack on 25 April 2007 while trying to put out a bonfire at his home.

6. Wally Barnes

Barnes spent a dozen years at Highbury and in January 1967 became manager of Highland Park in South Africa.

7. Geoff Barnett

Arsenal's long-serving but perennially unlucky reserve goalie left the club in January 1976 and in 1981 went on to become briefly coach-manager of Minnesota Kicks in the North American Soccer League.

8. John Barnwell

Managed Peterborough United, Wolverhampton Wanderers, AEK Athens, Notts County and Walsall.

9. Pat Beasley

He managed Bristol City, Birmingham City and Dover Athletic.

10. Charlie Bell

Bell played only once for Arsenal – but scored twice. He became boss of Wigan Borough, Mansfield Town, Bournemouth & Boscombe Athletic and also worked in Italy, Portugal, Brazil and France.

11. Jeff Blockley

Never settled in as Frank McLintock's replacement, Blockley became boss of Leicester United, Shepshed Charterhouse and Hinckley Athletic.

12. Jimmy Bloomfield

Bloomfield was player-manager of Leyton Orient before spending six years at Filbert Street in charge of Leicester City. In September 1977, he returned to the Orient for a four-year spell in charge – until Thursday 27 August 1981. He was the boss when Arsenal beat Orient 3-0 at Stamford Bridge in the FA Cup Semi Final on Saturday 8 April 1978.

13. Dave Bowen

After nine years at Arsenal, Bowen joined Northampton Town in July 1959 as player-manager for ten months. He stayed on as manager for a further nine years before moving upstairs to become secretary and then general manager prior to his retirement in June 1986. From 1964 until 1974, he was part-time manager of Wales.

14. Frank Bradshaw

Bradshaw joined Arsenal in June 1914 and retired in May 1923. In those nine years, he made more than 130 league appearances plus 129 in wartime fixtures. On his retirement, he became manager of Aberdare Athletic but was unable to do much for the club and left eleven months later.

15. Liam Brady

After retiring from playing the game, Brady became manager of Celtic (19 June 1991-7 October 1993) and Brighton and Hove Albion (15 December 1993-20 November 1995), although neither appointment brought him the kind of success that he had enjoyed on the playing field. He rejoined Arsenal in July 1996, as Head of Youth Development and Academy Director.

16. Jimmy Brain

Born in Bristol, Brain was manager of King's Lynn in 1935 and Cheltenham Town in August 1937. After his retirement in May 1948, he returned to Highbury as a scout.

17. Laurie Brown

After playing for north London rivals Arsenal and Spurs, Brown was player-manager of Bradford Park Avenue and King's Lynn before becoming manager of Stockton.

18. Tony Burns

Goalie Tony Burns played for more than a dozen clubs in his career. He became manager of Tonbridge United in 1979.

19. John Butler

Butler signed professional terms with Arsenal in March 1914 only for the First World War to break out five months later. He served in France with the Royal Field Artillery during the conflict. He also played in two wartime matches for Arsenal and scored four times. Back in red after the war, he stayed at the club for a dozen years. On his retirement from playing, he became manager of Torquay United, Crystal Palace, Darling FC of Brussels and Colchester United. He was also coach of the Belgian national side for seven years until April 1939.

20. Ted Carr

He was manager of Darlington and Tow Law Town.

21. Stan Charlton

He succeeded Frank O'Farrell as manager of Weymouth in July 1965 and held the job for seven years until May 1972.

22. Archie Clark

He was manager of Gillingham for almost 19 years from 1 August 1939 until 30 June 1958.

23. Tommy Coakley

The former Arsenal winger managed Malden Town, Bishop's Stortford, Walsall (1 August 1986-27 December 1986) and Blakenhall Town.

24. Ernest "Tim" Coleman

Player-manager of Linby Colliery and two spells each as manager and caretaker manager of Notts County.

25. John "Tim" Coleman

He managed Maidstone United before moving to a continental coaching job in Holland.

26. Freddie Cox

He managed Bournemouth & Boscombe Athletic (April 1956-July 1958), Portsmouth (August 1958-February 1961), Gillingham (June 1962-April 1965) and Bournemouth (April 1965-April 1970) before running his own newsagents. He died in 1973.

27. Jack Crayston

After leaving the manager's chair at Arsenal in May 1958, he took over at Doncaster Rovers in July 1958 where he stayed for three years until he changed careers and ran a newsagent. He died in 1992.

28. George Curtis

In 13 years at Highbury, George Curtis played only 13 games (excluding wartime appearances). He managed Brighton & Hove Albion, Stevenage Town and various teams in Norway.

29. Bob Davidson

Manager of Redditch United for one season, Davidson was previously player-manager of Rugby Town.

30. John Devine

He was manager of Shelbourne for a short period in 1989.

31. Tommy Docherty

Often controversial, always witty, The Doc played for Arsenal between August 1958 and February 1961 when he left to become player-coach at Chelsea. In September of 1961, he replaced former Arsenal legend Ted Drake as manager at Stamford Bridge but in his first season in charge Chelsea were relegated. The team, nicknamed Docherty's Diamonds, went back to the First Division at the first attempt. In 1965, Chelsea won the League Cup beating Leicester City. Two years later, on Saturday 20 May 1967, he led Chelsea to the FA Cup Final but they lost 2-1 to Spurs. In October 1967, Docherty resigned as Chelsea boss and was replaced by former Arsenal coach Dave Sexton. In November 1967, Docherty became manager of Rotherham United but fell out with his board of directors and left in 1968. That year he became manager of Queens Park Rangers but left after 29 days. He then spent 13 months from December 1968 as manager at Aston Villa. On Monday 19 January 1970, as Villa languished at the foot of the Second Division, The Doc was sacked. Next in February 1970 he moved to FC Porto. On Friday 2 July 1971, Docherty was appointed assistant manager to Terry Neill at Hull City. Just over two months later, on Sunday 12 September he became caretaker manager of Scotland, with the job becoming permanent in November. In December 1972, the board of Manchester United sacked Frank O'Farrell and on the twenty-second of that month appointed The Doc as the new manager. In 1973-74, United were relegated from the First Division but bounced back in a year. In 1976, Docherty led United to the FA Cup Final but they lost to Southampton. The following year, they won the trophy beating Liverpool. News broke that Docherty was having an affair with the wife of United physio Laurie Brown and the manager was sacked on Sunday 3 July 1977. Former Arsenal coach Dave Sexton again replaced him. From Saturday 17 September 1977 until Thursday 10 May 1979, Docherty was manager at Derby County.

In May 1979, he joined Queens Park Rangers but was quickly sacked and then reinstated after just nine days. In October 1980, he was sacked again, later saying, "I sacked Queens Park Rangers once and they later sacked me twice." In 1981, he briefly managed Sydney Olympic in Australia. Back in England, he was in charge of Preston North End for a few months ("They offered me a handshake of £10,000 to settle amicably. I told them they would have to be a lot more amicable than that") before returning down under to boss South Melbourne Hellas. In 1983, he had another spell at Sydney Olympic. From Friday 8 June 1984 until Thursday 4 July 1985 he was manager at Wolverhampton Wanderers and then at Altrincham from 1987 until his retirement in 1988. Among his better-known quips are "The ideal board of directors should be made up of three men, two dead and one dying" and "Preston are one of my old clubs, but then most of them are. I've had more clubs than Jack Nicklaus."

32. Bill Dodgin

He managed Queens Park Rangers, Fulham, Northampton Town (twice), Brentford and Woking.

33. Ted Drake

The Arsenal legend became manager of Hendon in August 1946, then spent five years at Reading before moving to Stamford Bridge where he was in charge from June 1952 until September 1961. Tommy Docherty (see above) replaced him. He died in 1995.

34. George Eastham, OBE

In February 1971, Eastham became manager of South African side Hellenic FC. Six years later, he took over as manager of Stoke City, the team he joined in August 1966 from Arsenal. He was in charge from March 1977 until January 1978.

35. Mike Everitt

He managed Brentford for 16 months in the mid-Seventies.

36. Gordon Ferry

He replaced fellow ex-Gunner Gerry Ward as manager of Barnet in May 1969.

37. Alex Forbes

In the 1960s, this former Gunner became manager of Johannesburg Rangers in South Africa.

38. Bobby Gould

Gould managed Bristol Rovers, Wimbledon, West Bromwich Albion, Coventry City, Queens Park Rangers, Cheltenham Town and the Wales national side.

39. George Graham

Managed Millwall, Arsenal, leading the club to two League titles, Leeds United and Spurs.

40. Arfon Griffiths, MBE

He was player-manager, then manager of Wrexham and then had a brief spell in charge at Crewe Alexandra.

41. David Halliday

He was player manager of Yeovil Town, manager of Aberdeen for almost 18 years (December 1937-1955) and finally manager of Leicester City after which he retired from football. Halliday and Alex Ferguson are the only two managers to bring the championship title to Aberdeen. He died in 1970.

42. Eddie Hapgood

Former Gunner Hapgood managed Blackburn Rovers (June 1946-February 1947), Watford from February 1948 to March 1950, and Bath City (March 1950-February 1956).

43. Jimmie Harvey

The ex-midfielder managed Morecambe for two years.

44. Martin Hayes

He has been manager of Bishop's Stortford since 1999.

45. Leslie Henley

He was player manager of Irish side Bohemians and later coach-manager of Wimbledon for 16 years when they were a non-league side.

46. David Herd

Herd was briefly in charge of Lincoln City.

47. Frank Hill

He was player-manager of Crewe Alexandra, then in charge at Burnley, Preston North End, Notts County and Charlton Athletic.

48. David Hillier

Now retired, Hillier works as a fireman in Bristol and manages Oldland Abbotonians in the Western Divison One.

49. John Hollins, MBE

Hollins was manager for three years at Chelsea from Tuesday 11 June 1985, a club where he had spent 14 years as a player. He was sacked in March 1988. On Tuesday 11 November 1997 he became caretaker manager at Queens Park Rangers after Stewart Houston was sacked. From July 1998 until Wednesday 12 September 2001, he was manager of Swansea City. On Tuesday 11 December 2001, he was appointed manager of Rochdale but left after five months. He was caretaker manager of Stockport County for four weeks in 2003 and in November 2005 became manager of Crawley Town.

50. Don Howe

Howe managed West Bromwich Albion, Arsenal, Queens Park Rangers and Coventry City.

51. Joe Hulme

Hulme managed deadly rivals Spurs for almost four years.

52. John Hunter

Known as "Sailor" Hunter, he was manager of Motherwell for 35 years (April 1911-May 1946) after leaving Woolwich Arsenal in May 1905. He then became Motherwell's secretary until his retirement in August 1959 at the age of 80. The club granted him a weekly pension upon his retirement. He died at Motherwell on 12 January 1966.

53. David Jack

He managed Southend United, Middlesbrough and Shelbourne.

54. John Jensen

He managed Danish side Herfolge for two years after hanging up his boots. More recently, he has been turning out for Arsenal's over-35s side. Playing for the first team, he scored just one goal in 138 appearances – it came on a cold and wet 31 December 1994 after 98 matches, against Queens Park Rangers.

55. George Jobey

The first player to score for Woolwich Arsenal at Highbury, Jobey was also the first player to be carried off injured (on a milk cart). His first goal was against Leicester Fosse and when they became Leicester City (in 1919) he joined them. He became player-manager of Northampton Town, manager of Wolverhampton Wanderers, Derby County and finally Mansfield Town. He died on 9 May 1962.

56. Bob John

He was assistant manager (to ex-Gunner Jack Butler) at Crystal Palace for two years at the end of the Forties. In 1950, he was manager of Torquay United for eight months.

57. Charlie Jones

He managed Notts County but did not meet with too much success at Meadow Lane leaving after seven months. He was more successful as non-league Crittalls Athletic's secretary-manager and, by all accounts, took coaching sessions in his slippers.

58. Leslie Jones

Player-manager of Barry Town, he later resumed playing only duties (for Brighton & Hove Albion) before taking the managerial reins at Scunthorpe United and Lindsey United.

59. Eddie Kelly

The first substitute to score in an FA Cup Final became manager of Barnstaple Town in June 1995.

60. Noel Kelly

He was successively player-manager of Tranmere Rovers and Ellesmere Port Town before he became boss at Holyhead Town.

61. Brian Kidd

Assistant manager at Manchester United, Kidd left amid some ill feeling to take the top job at Blackburn Rovers.

62. John Kosmina

After a very brief career at Highbury, Kosmina returned to his native Australia. Following his retirement, he became manager (1995) of Warringah Dolphins in the New South Wales Soccer League. In 1997 he moved to Newcastle Breakers and then Brisbane Strikers, Adelaide United and on 24 October 2007 he took over at Sydney FC.

63. Jack Lambert

He was player-boss for Margate before returning to Arsenal as a coach.

64. Tommy Lawton

In 1953, Lawton had a brief spell as manager of Brentford. In November 1953, he returned to playing with Arsenal for a fee of £10,000 In February 1956, he left Arsenal to become player-manager of Kettering Town. He then moved to Notts County as manager before returning for another spell as manager at Kettering.

65. Ned Liddell

He was player-manager of Southend United and then manager of Queens Park Rangers and Luton Town before finally becoming a scout for Spurs.

66. Jimmy Logie

He was player-manager of Gravesend and Northfleet after spending 16 years at Highbury.

67. Archie Macaulay

He was player-manager of Guildford City and then managed Norwich City, West Bromwich Albion and Brighton & Hove Albion before taking the bizarre decision to become a traffic warden.

68. Malcolm Macdonald

Macdonald managed Fulham for four years. He later took the helm at Huddersfield Town between 1987 and 1988.

69. Sandy MacFarlane

He was secretary-manager of Dundee for six years before occupying the same position at Charlton Athletic for two and a half years. In January 1928 he spent another six months as manager at Dundee before returning to The Valley as secretary-manager for another four and a half years.

70. Eddie McGill

He managed Fredrikshavn in Denmark for two years in the early 1970s.

71. Eddie McGoldrick

He spent three seasons at Highbury and finally retired from football in 1999. He was player-manager of Corby Town in 2000 and then manager of Bashley in 2003.

72. Billy McCullough

In July 1968, he became player-manager of Cork City and then manager of Derry City.

73. Ian McKechnie

In March 1978, he spent a fortnight as manager of Nuneaton Borough and then two years as manager of Sligo Rovers.

74. Angus McKinnon

He became manager of Wigan Borough having previously occupied the position of trainer. He then became manager of Connah's Quay.

75. Frank McLintock, MBE

He became manager of Leicester City but in his one season in charge, they were relegated from the First Division. Between 1984 and 1987, he was boss of Brentford.

76. Joe Mercer, MBE

Mercer was manager of Sheffield United (18 August 1955-December 1958), Aston Villa (December 1958-July 1964 – he was sacked as he was recovering from a stroke), Manchester City (1965-1972) and Coventry City (1972-1975) and was caretaker manager of England after Sir Alf Ramsey's resignation.

77. Paul Merson

He was manager at Walsall until his sacking on 6 February 2006.

78. Jackie Mordue

For a year, he was player-manager of Durham City.

79. Steve Morrow

After leaving Arsenal, Morrow moved to Queens Park Rangers before ending his career with FC Dallas. When he retired because of a neck injury, he became assistant coach at the club. On 11 December 2006 he was appointed manager. He was sacked on Tuesday 20 May 2008 two days after FC Dallas lost 5-1 at home to David Beckham's Los Angeles Galaxy.

80. Frank Moss

After retiring from keeping goal for Arsenal, Moss became manager of Heart of Midlothian where he spent three years.

81. Terry Neill

He managed Hull City, Northern Ireland, Spurs and Arsenal.

82. David Nelson

He was player-manager of Ashford Town until he emigrated to the United States of America.

83. David O'Leary

In October 1998, he became manager of Leeds United succeeding George Graham but was sacked in 2002 after failing to get results. Terry Venables who had once been mooted as a potential manager for Arsenal replaced him. In June 2003, O'Leary became boss at Aston Villa but was sacked in July 2006. He wrote a book about his time at Elland Road *Leeds United: A Season On Trial: The Inside Story of an Astonishing Year.*

84. Tom Parker

Former Gunner Parker managed Southampton for six years before becoming a surveyor. Returning to football, he managed Norwich City for almost two years.

85. Colin Pates

He was player-manager of Crawley Town until 1996.

86. Vladimir Petrović

Petrović joined Arsenal from Red Star Belgrade in December 1982. In 1994, he became his former club's manager.

87. David Platt

After leaving Arsenal, he became player-coach/manager of Sampdoria in Italy and then in June 1999 player-manager of Nottingham Forest. On 17 July 2001, Platt became manager of the England under-21 side.

88. Richie Powling

He managed non-league Tiptree United and Sudbury Town.

89. Niall Quinn, MBE

Quinn bought a controlling stake in Sunderland on 3 July 2006 and appointed himself chairman and manager. He made way as manager for Roy Keane. Phenomenally generous, Quinn gave the £1million profits from his testimonial game to charity and when Sunderland fans were stranded in Bristol when an overzealous pilot refused to fly, he paid £8,000 for taxis to take the fans home.

90. John Radford

He managed Bishop's Stortford, the club later bossed by fellow Arsenal old boy Martin Hayes.

91. Graham Rix

Rix was manager of Portsmouth from 25 February 2001 until 25 March 2002. He became manager of Oxford United on 22 March 2004 but was sacked and replaced by Harry Redknapp. From 8 November 2005 until 22 March 2006, he was manager of Heart of Midlothian. He was sacked after four months when the chairman announced his dissatisfaction with the team's results.

92. John Roberts

The ex-Arsenal defender was player-manager of Oswestry Town for almost two years.

93. Ronnie Rooke

He was player-manager at Crystal Palace for 17 months and then he had two spells as player-manager at Bedford Town (February 1951-May 1955 and August 1959-October 1961).

94. Wilf Rostron

After one day as caretaker manager of Gateshead, he spent six months in charge of Ryhope Colliery Welfare.

95. Laurie Scott

He became player-manager at Crystal Palace for three years before he was appointed manager at Hendon followed by a stint as boss of Hitchin Town.

96. Paddy Sloan

The Irish international became player-manager of Lockheed Leamington in January 1956.

97. Lionel Smith

Smith was appointed manager of Gravesend and Northfleet for two years in the 1950s.

98. Rodney Smithson

Smithson who made just two appearances in five years at Highbury in the early Sixties was player-manager at Whitney Town for three and a half years.

99. Brian Sparrow

He was manager of Crawley Town between 1988 and 1992.

100. Frank Stapleton

Ex-forward Stapleton became player-manager of Bradford City for two and a half years and then spent 16 months as boss of New England Teamen in America.

101. George Swindin

Player-manager of Peterborough United and then Swindin managed Arsenal, Norwich City and Cardiff City.

102. Brian Talbot

He managed West Bromwich Albion from November 1988 until January 1991. He then was in charge at Aldershot (February–November 1991), Hibernians (the team won the Maltese Premier League in 1993 and 1994 under his stewardship). He led Rushden & Diamonds into the Football League during five years in charge (1999-2004), before taking over at Oldham Athletic (2004-March 2005), Oxford United (May 2005-March 2006) and Marsaxlokk, again in Malta.

103. Mike Tiddy

He was player-manager of non-league Penzance for two years before becoming a village postmaster.

104. Ian Ure

For a year, he managed East Stirlingshire replacing Sir Alex Ferguson.

105. Steve Walford

Briefly manager at Wealdstone, he has carved a position as assistant to Martin O'Neill, working with him at five clubs.

106. Gerry Ward

He managed Barnet from September 1967 until May 1969 when he was replaced by ex-Gunner Gordon Ferry.

107. Charlie Williams

He managed the Danish club B93 and French side Lille OSC.

108. George Wood

He managed Inter Cardiff, in the Welsh Second Division, from 1995 until 1997.

THE THINGS THEY SAY – XI

"Arsenal will be in my blood as well as my heart. I said I was going to be a Gunner life and I didn't lie because when you are a Gunner you will always be a Gunner."

Thierry Henry explains leaving Arsenal,
after saying he will always stay there, 2007

UP FOR THE CUP – VIII

Arsenal 1 Swindon Town 3

A year on from the defeat by Leeds and Arsenal were back at Wembley in the League Cup Final. On Saturday 15 March 1969, their opponents were Third Division Swindon Town before 98,169 fans. Arsenal were expected to win easily but not for the first time the minnows upset the form book and after extra time ran out 3-1 winners. Bobby Gould scored Arsenal's goal. The main consolation was that because Swindon were a Third Division side they were not allowed to take up their prize as participants in the European Fairs Cup so Arsenal who wore gold and blue for the match were given their place. Arsenal: Bob Wilson, Peter Storey, Bob McNab, Frank McLintock (captain), Ian Ure, Peter Simpson (George Graham), John Radford, Jon Sammels, Bobby Gould, David Court, George Armstrong.

CAPTAINS FANTASTIC

The following men lifted the league championship trophy for the club.

Tom Parker 1930–31
Eddie Hapgood 1932–33, 1933–34, 1934–35, 1937–38
Joe Mercer 1947–48, 1952–53
Frank McLintock 1970–71
Tony Adams 1988–89, 1990–91, 1997–98, 2001–02
Patrick Vieira 2003–04

STARS IN THEIR EYES

On 21 November 2007, the International Astronomical Union revealed that asteroid 33179 had been renamed Arsène Wenger. Ian Griffin discovered the asteroid and his citation read: "Asteroid 33179 Arsenewenger is named to honour the achievements of Arsène Wenger, a French football manager, who has been manager of Arsenal FC in England since 1996. He is the club's most successful manager in terms of trophies won. In 2004, he became the only manager in Premier League history to go through an entire season undefeated. Wenger's teams are renowned for their beautiful approach to the game. The asteroid orbits between Mars and Jupiter taking 4.23 years to complete one circuit of the sun."

BYE BYE CASHLEY

One of the best left-backs to have played for Arsenal in recent years was Ashley Cole who made his debut on 30 November 1999 against Middlesbrough. Three months later, on 25 February 2000, he signed professional terms. On 14 May 2000 he made his first appearance for Arsenal in the Premier League in a match against Newcastle United. During his time at Arsenal he won two league championship medals and three FA Cup winner's medals as well as a runner's up medal for the Champions League. In all, he made 228 first-team appearances for the Gunners and scored nine goals. In January 2005 he had illegal talks with Chelsea manager José Mourinho, chief executive, Peter Kenyon about a move to Stamford Bridge and when the news came out he declared, "I wouldn't play for Arsenal again even for £200,000 a week." On 2 June 2005 the Premier League fined Cole £100,000 (later reduced to £75,000). Six weeks after this outburst, on 18 July 2005 he signed a new contract at Arsenal. Arsène Wenger commented, "If people come to your window and talk to your wife every night, you can't accept it without asking what's happening." It was not the end of the matter. A year later, Cole published his non-best-selling autobiography, *My Defence*, and attacked Arsenal: "When I heard the figure of £55k I nearly swerved off the road, I yelled down the phone, 'He's taking the piss Jonathan [Barnett, Cole's agent].' I was so incensed, I was trembling with anger." The cause of this fury was Arsène Wenger's refusal to pay Cole £60,000 a week. On 31 August 2006 Cole joined Chelsea for £5million plus William Gallas leading Cole to be nicknamed "Cashley Cole". When Arsenal met Chelsea at Stamford Bridge on 12 December 2006 some Arsenal fans had had fake Bank of Cashley £20 notes printed to wave at the ex-Gunner. In a typically ridiculous over-reaction the Metropolitan Police Force announced it would arrest anyone seen with the "money". For his part, Cole said, "I am genuine. It's never been about money. For me it's about respect."

TV COMMENTATOR WHO BECAME A LINESMAN

On 16 September 1972 Arsenal were playing host to Liverpool at Highbury when linesman Dennis Drewitt was injured. TV presenter Jimmy Hill came down from the commentary box and ran the line for the rest of the match which ended goalless.

TOP TEN SCORERS – BY SEASON

These are the highest individual scorers per season for Arsenal.

1. Reg Lewis...................47.......................1942-43
2. Ted Drake..................45.......................1934-35
2. Reg Lewis...................45.......................1941-42
4. Leslie Compton..........42.......................1940-41
5. Jimmy Brain ....39.......................1925-26
5. Jack Lambert ....39.......................1930-31
5. Thierry Henry.............39.......................2003-04
8. Ian Wright..................35.......................1993-94
9. Jimmy Brain ....34.......................1926-27
9. Ronnie Rooke ....34.......................1947-48

ARSENAL'S TOP MEN

David O'Leary was born in Stoke Newington, London on Friday 2 May 1958. He has played for Arsenal more times than any other player. He joined the club in June 1973 and turned professional in July 1975. He made his debut away to Burnley on Saturday 16 August 1975. By the time of his last season (1992-93), he had pulled on an Arsenal shirt 523 times with a further 35 appearances as a sub. It was not until 1990-91 that he first came on a substitute. He scored 11 goals. In total, O'Leary played for Arsenal 1,005 times at league, FA Cup, League Cup, European, friendly, tour, Football Combination, South East Counties, and youth levels. Ray Parlour has made the most appearances in the Premier League. Born in Romford, Essex, on Wednesday 7 March 1973, he joined Arsenal as a schoolboy in January 1988 and became a trainee in July 1989. He turned pro in March 1991 and made his debut at Anfield against Liverpool on Wednesday 29 January 1992. In his Arsenal career, Parlour played 333 Premier League games. Tom Parker was born in Woolston, Hampshire, on 19 November 1897. A right-back, he joined Arsenal in March 1926 from Southampton. The first Arsenal captain to hold aloft a trophy, Parker made the most consecutive appearances for the club. He made his debut on Saturday 3 April 1926 (4-2 home win against Blackburn Rovers) between then and Thursday 26 December 1929 (a 2-1 home defeat by Portsmouth), he played 172 times for the Gunners.

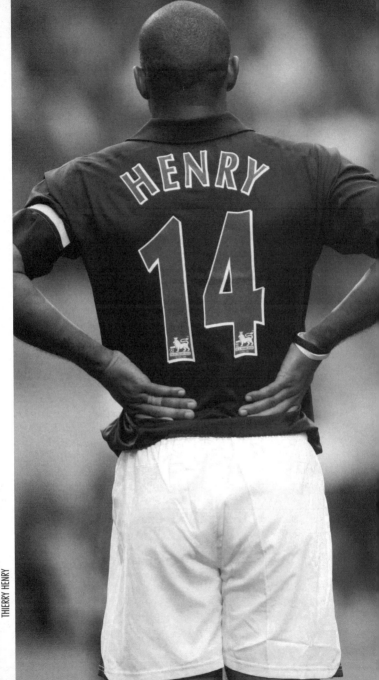

UP FOR THE CUP – IX

Anderlecht 3 Arsenal 1

Thanks to Swindon Town's ineligibility Arsenal entered the European Inter Cities Fairs Cup and battled their way through to the two-legged final against RSC Anderlecht. The first leg was played at the Parc Astrid in Belgium on Wednesday 22 April 1970 before 37,000 fans. The Belgian club won by a comfortable (or so they thought) 3-1 with substitute Ray Kennedy getting one back for the Gunners. Kennedy had only played twice for the first team prior to the game and had made two further appearances as a substitute. Frank McLintock was desolate thinking that he would end up on the losing side of a cup final again but for the second leg he geed up the team before kick-off telling them that they could win. Arsenal: Bob Wilson, Peter Storey, Bob McNab, Frank McLintock (captain), Peter Simpson, Eddie Kelly, George Graham, George Armstrong, Jon Sammels, John Radford, Charlie George (Ray Kennedy).

Arsenal 3 Anderlecht 0

Six days later before 51,612 spectators at Highbury the teams met again. Glaswegian Eddie Kelly opened Arsenal's account from 25 yards with less than half an hour on the clock and later said, "I could have jumped out of the stadium when I saw it go into the top of the net." The goal invigorated the team and the crowd began to get even more behind them than usual. John Radford made it 2-0 from a Bob McNab cross which was enough to give them the trophy. On the 71st minute, Charlie George passed to Jon Sammels and he put it away to make it 3-0 and 4-3 on aggregate, gaining Arsenal their first European trophy and first trophy since Joe Mercer's men in 1953. Arsenal: Bob Wilson, Peter Storey, Bob McNab, Frank McLintock (captain), Peter Simpson, Eddie Kelly, George Graham, George Armstrong, Jon Sammels, John Radford, Charlie George.

THE SHAMING OF ENGLAND

On Monday 14 May 1938, England played Germany in a friendly in Berlin. As the players lined up before the game, under orders from the FA, the England team – including Arsenal players Eddie Hapgood who was captain and Cliff Bastin – shamefully gave the Nazi salute. England won 6-3 with one of the goals from Cliff Bastin.

UP FOR THE CUP – X

Arsenal 2 Liverpool 1 (aet)

FA Cup Final fever hit north London in May 1971 when Arsenal met Liverpool for the second time in the final and Arsenal sniffed the possibility of winning their first double. The teams met on Saturday 8 May 1971 before a full house of 100,000 at Wembley with Arsenal wearing their change strip of gold and blue with Liverpool in their familiar all red. Arsenal ran out 2-1 winners after a heat-sapping extra time with the goals from Eddie Kelly and Charlie George. Years later, Peter Thompson of Liverpool recalled Bill Shankly's pre-match team talk. "He really didn't give Arsenal any credit. He said, 'They're nothing to beat, these Cockneys from London.'" Arsenal: Bob Wilson, Pat Rice, Bob McNab, Peter Storey (Eddie Kelly), Frank McLintock (captain), Peter Simpson, George Armstrong, George Graham, John Radford, Ray Kennedy, Charlie George.

A LOUGHBOROUGH DOZEN

On Monday 12 March 1900, Arsenal achieved their biggest ever win in the league beating Loughborough Town 12-0 in the Second Division. Despite the glut of goals, only 900 people turned up to watch. Gaudie (3), Cottrell (2), Dick (2), Main (2), Tennant (2) and a solo effort from Anderson, were the goalscorers. Woolwich Arsenal: Roger Ord, Duncan McNichol, James Jackson, James Moir, John Dick, John Anderson, Fergus Hunt, Peter Logan, Ralph Gaudie, Andrew McCowie, James Tennant.

KEEPING IT IN THE FAMILY

Denis and Leslie Compton are the only brothers to have played in the same Arsenal side. Perry Groves (George Graham's first signing as manager) and uncle Vic Groves both played for the club although never at the same time. David Neave and his younger brother Andrew were both on Arsenal's books although Andrew never made the first team. Behind the scenes physio Gary Lewin worked with his cousin Colin until the former left the club in the summer of 2008. The son of another Arsenal trainer, Billy Milne, William Junior played for Arsenal as a youngster.

THE BATTLE OF HIGHBURY

On Wednesday 14 November 1934, Highbury was the venue for an international between England and Italy. The England side had seven Arsenal players and Italy had just recently won their second World Cup. It promised to be a thrilling encounter. The Football Association had not entered an England side to the World Cups in 1930 and 1934 and would not enter the 1938 competition believing that England would win anyway and it was beneath them to mix with Johnny Foreigner. Italian dictator Benito Mussolini was convinced that the World Cup victory was a triumph for fascism and that a victory against England would cement his beliefs. England and, for that matter, Arsenal's reputation did precede them. A European diplomat recalled "It was said that if you asked a European schoolboy the question 'Who is Bastin?' he would reply, 'Outside left for the Arsenal, the greatest club side in the world.' However, ask the same child who is Winston Churchill and he would say, 'I am sorry I do not know that player.'" Such was the atmosphere as the Italians arrived at Arsenal Stadium for the match. Added to the tension was the news from Rome that Mussolini had promised the Italian players limitless wealth if they won – well, a bonus 0f £150, a new Alfa Romeo and exemption from national service. England? They received the princely sum of £2. The England team, before 56,044 spectators that day, was: Frank Moss (Arsenal), George Male (Arsenal), Eddie Hapgood (Arsenal), Cliff Britton (Everton), Jack Barker (Derby County), Wilf Copping (Arsenal), Stanley Matthews (Stoke City), Ray Bowden (Arsenal), Ted Drake (Arsenal), Cliff Bastin (Arsenal), and Eric Brook (Manchester City). The Italians fielded Carlo Ceresoli (Ambrosiana-Inter), Eraldo Monzeglio (Bologna), Luigi Allemandi (Ambrosiana-Inter), Attilio Ferraris (AS Roma), Luis Monti (Juventus), Luigi Bertolini (Juventus), Enrique Guaita (AS Roma), Pietro Serantoni (Juventus), Giuseppe Meazza (Ambrosiana-Inter), Giovanni Ferrari (Juventus) and Raimundo Orsi (Juventus). George Allison, the secretary-manager of Arsenal, provided radio commentary and Arsenal trainer Tom Whittaker doubled up as the England man with the magic sponge. The two teams had met only once before – 18 months earlier in Rome when the result was a 1–1 draw. Italy had been beaten only four times in 34 matches since Vittorio Pozzo took over as manager in late 1929 after two brief earlier stints in the role for the

Olympic Games of 1912 and 1924. Italy were at full strength, making only two changes from their World Cup-winning team. Carlo Ceresoli, who missed the World Cup through injury but would become the first-choice goalkeeper for the year following it, replaced veteran Giuseppe Combi, and inside forward Pietro Serantoni, who would become a regular in the team and play in the 1938 World Cup final match, replaced Angelo Schiavio. At the other end of the pitch, the England team was inexperienced – none of the players had more than nine caps to their credit then. Arsenal's George Male and Eddie Hapgood were making their international debuts that day. The honoured guest at Highbury was Prince Arthur of Connaught, Queen Victoria's third son, and the match kicked off on a foggy, wet afternoon. Officiating was Otto Olsson, Sweden assisted by the linesmen Mr L. E. Gibbs, from the Buckinghamshire & Berkshire FA, and Signor J. De Rensis from Genoa. In the first minute of play, Ceresoli fouled Drake and Mr Olsson awarded a penalty to England. Eric Brook stood up to take the penalty but Ceresoli saved it. A minute later, Italian centre-half Monti broke a bone in his foot after a challenge from Ted Drake and had to leave the pitch. The Italians were down to ten men and they did not like it a bit. The tackling became fiercer and fiercer. After three minutes, Eric Brook put England ahead and seven minutes late added a second to England's account. Hapgood, making his debut as England captain, had to leave the pitch for 15 minutes with a broken nose courtesy of an Italian elbow. During his absence, and with just 12 minutes on the clock, Ted Drake put England 3-0 up and that was still the score at half time. The second half began as the rain worsened and, with 58 minutes gone, Italy's brilliant centre-forward Giuseppe "Peppino" Meazza pulled one back. Buoyed by the goal, Italy pushed forward and began playing some skilful football. The brilliance of Frank Moss, in his last international appearance, kept England ahead although he could do nothing on the 62nd minute when Meazza scored to make the score 3-2. That was the way it finished although the treatment tables of both dressing rooms were full. Other England players who were hurt and needed Tom Whittaker's magic sponge included Eric Brook, who suffered a broken arm, Ray Bowden (ankle injury), Jack Barker (hand strapped) and Ted Drake (cut leg). Hapgood was later to comment in his autobiography, "It's a bit hard to play when somebody resembling an enthusiastic member of the mafia is scraping his studs down your leg."

THE BATTLE OF GOODISON PARK

In the 1930s, the Arsenal reigned supreme on the pitch and, as every team needs a hard man, Arsenal's was Wilf "Iron Man" Copping. On Saturday 16 March 1935, the club travelled to Liverpool to play Everton before a crowd of 50,389. The game started and quickly the home crowd began to shout at the Arsenal players labelling them "southern poofs". Copping was not pleased – initially because he came from Yorkshire but also because he hated to hear his team mates insulted. Within five minutes of the start of the second half, Copping took out Everton's Jack Coulter who had been amused by the crowd's chanting. Fellow Evertonian Will Creswell was furious and decided to get his revenge. On 70 minutes, he and Copping went for the same ball and Creswell split open the Arsenal man's shinpad. Five minutes later, Copping tackled Creswell and sent the Toffeeman over the hoarding and onto the terrace. Four foolhardy Everton fans decided that Copping had gone too far and threatened the Arsenal left half. Copping informed them that he had a football match to finish but would be more than happy to entertain them afterwards. Moss and Drake scored as Arsenal ran out 2-0 winners. When Copping went to find his tormentors, they had fled.

UP FOR THE CUP – XI

Arsenal 0 Leeds United 1

Arsenal returned to Wembley on Saturday 6 May 1972 to meet the team that had deprived them of the League Cup four years earlier. It was to be the same result with Leeds winning 1-0 before 100,000 people. Arsenal: Geoff Barnett, Pat Rice, Bob McNab, Peter Storey, Frank McLintock (captain), Peter Simpson, George Armstrong, Alan Ball, Charlie George, John Radford (Ray Kennedy), George Graham.

BIG SPENDER

Dr Leigh Richmond "Dicky" Roose was educated by H.G. Wells and later trained as a doctor at King's College Hospital, London. Before the days of huge pay packets, he thought nothing of splashing the cash and often took a taxi to the ground rather than the bus used by the rest of the team. He was killed in action during the First World War.

LET THERE BE LIGHT

In 1930, Arsenal's visionary manager Herbert Chapman paid a visit to Belgium and watched a match under floodlights. He immediately saw a potential new way to expand the game. Chapman arranged for lights to be installed at Highbury both for the main pitch and the practice one. However, the footballing authorities refused to let them be used for league matches. It would not be until 1951 that a game was first placed under floodlights at Highbury. On Wednesday 17 October 1951, Arsenal played Hapoel Tel Aviv and later the same year played Rangers also under lights. It was 1956 before lights became a fixture at football grounds.

ARSENAL AVERTS TRAGEDY

On 27 November 1938, Arsenal's first team flew on two planes to Paris to play Racing Club in what was becoming a traditional fixture. The aircraft took off from Croydon but when they came in to land at Le Bourget thick fog had enveloped the French capital. The first plane landed safely but as the second came into land the pilot realised he would not be able to so he pushed in the throttle to give the plane some power and it soared back into the air – missing the first aircraft and certain death by only a few feet. Even then, the plane was not out of danger. As it rose, the plane narrowly avoided a hangar before gaining height. He circled and came back in safely. The players jumped into taxis for the game. The result was 1-1.

TOP TEN SCORERS – BY CAREER

Player	Goals	Games	Average
1. Thierry Henry	226	370	0.61
2. Ian Wright	185	288	0.64
3. Cliff Bastin	178	395	0.45
4. John Radford	149	475	0.31
5. Ted Drake	139	184	0.76
6. Jimmy Brain	139	232	0.60
7. Doug Lishman	137	244	0.56
8. Joe Hulme	125	374	0.33
9. David Jack	124	208	0.60
10. Dennis Bergkamp	121	423	0.29

UP FOR THE CUP – XII

Arsenal 0 Ipswich Town 1

Six years to the day after they lost 1-0 to Leeds United in the FA Cup Final Arsenal returned to Wembley on Saturday 6 May 1978 to meet Ipswich Town. double-winning manager Bertie Mee had left the club and Terry Neill was facing his first of three consecutive FA Cup finals. One hundred thousand people saw Paul Mariner and George Burley almost score for the Tractor Boys but the woodwork and Pat Jennings saved Arsenal. After 76 minutes, Ipswich attacked and Willie Young miss-hit his clearance, the ball landing at the feet of Roger Osborne who belted it past Jennings to take the cup by the now familiar score line of 1-0. Pat Rice was the only survivor from the 1972 Cup Final.

Arsenal: Pat Jennings, Pat Rice (captain), Sammy Nelson, David Price, David O'Leary, Willie Young, Liam Brady (Graham Rix), Alan Sunderland, Malcolm Macdonald, Frank Stapleton, Alan Hudson.

THE ARSENAL – DECADE BY DECADE: 1930s

1930-31

First Division	P	W	D	L	F	A	W	D	L	F	A	Pts
1. Arsenal	42	14	5	2	67	27	14	5	2	60	32	66

FA Cup: Fourth round

1931-32

First Division	P	W	D	L	F	A	W	D	L	F	A	Pts
2. Arsenal	42	14	5	2	52	16	8	5	8	38	32	54

FA Cup: Runners-up

1932-33

First Division	P	W	D	L	F	A	W	D	L	F	A	Pts
1. Arsenal	42	14	3	4	70	27	11	5	5	48	34	58

FA Cup: Third round

1933-34

First Division	P	W	D	L	F	A	W	D	L	F	A	Pts
1. Arsenal	42	15	4	2	45	19	10	5	6	30	28	59

FA Cup: Sixth round

1934-35

First Division	P	W	D	L	F	A	W	D	L	F	A	Pts
1. Arsenal	42	15	4	2	74	17	8	8	5	41	29	58

FA Cup: Sixth round

1935-36

First Division	P	W	D	L	F	A	W	D	L	F	A	Pts
6. Arsenal	42	9	9	3	44	22	6	6	9	34	26	45

FA Cup: Winners

1936-37

First Division	P	W	D	L	F	A	W	D	L	F	A	Pts
3. Arsenal	42	10	10	1	43	20	8	6	7	37	29	52

FA Cup: Sixth round

1937-38

First Division	P	W	D	L	F	A	W	D	L	F	A	Pts
1. Arsenal	42	15	4	2	52	16	6	6	9	25	28	52

FA Cup: Fifth round

1938-39

First Division	P	W	D	L	F	A	W	D	L	F	A	Pts
5. Arsenal	42	14	3	4	34	14	5	6	10	21	27	47

FA Cup: Third round

1939-1945 the Football League was suspended due to the Second World War.

PARLEZ-VOUS ANGLAIS?

On Monday 14 February 2005, Arsenal beat Crystal Palace 5-1 at Highbury. The Gunners team did not include one Englishman in the starting line-up. Arsène Wenger said, "When you work on the training ground every day, you don't notice where they're from. I don't even know where I'm from." Arsenal: Jens Lehmann (Germany), Lauren (Cameroon), Gaël Clichy (France), Patrick Vieira (France), Kolo Touré (Ivory Coast), Pascal Cygan (France), José Antonio Reyes (Spain), Edu (Brazil), Thierry Henry (France), Dennis Bergkamp (Holland) and Robert Pirès (France).

GUNNERS IN THE MEDIA

Arsenal led the way in involvement in media coverage with George Allison commenting on several matches on the wireless. He also began his career in local newspapers before joining Middlesbrough as assistant manager when he was 21. In 1906 he became the BBC's Woolwich Arsenal correspondent, later becoming London correspondent of the New York Herald as well as secretary, programme editor and club historian for Arsenal. In 1926, Allison became a director of Arsenal and the following year commentated on the 1927 FA Cup Final with Derek McCulloch, later to be children's entertainer Uncle Mac. These are some other more modern exponents of the media art.

Lee Dixon

Dixon made his Arsenal debut on Saturday 13 February 1988 in a 2-1 home victory over Luton Town. For the next 14 years, he was a regular in the number two shirt making 619 appearances for the club and scored 28 goals. On his retirement, he became in demand for his analysis of televised matches. His most recent job was analysing Euro 2008 for the BBC.

Malcolm Macdonald

He presents the Three Legends Football Phone-In with Bernie Slaven and Micky Horswill on local radio Century FM.

Bob McNab

McNab was one of the earliest television pundits; he worked for ITV during the 1970 World Cup Finals alongside Malcolm Allison, Derek Dougan and Paddy Crerand.

Bob Wilson

Before his retirement from Arsenal, Wilson worked as a pundit for the BBC during the 1970 World Cup. After leaving Highbury, he hosted *Football Focus* for the BBC from 1974 until 1994 when he moved to ITV where he stayed until his retirement in 2002. During his stint on Football Focus, he re-signed as emergency goalkeeper cover for Arsenal and worked as the club's goalkeeping coach.

Kenny Sansom

The former Arsenal and England full-back is the co-presenter of LBC Radio's Saturday afternoon football programme.

Ian Wright, MBE

Probably the ex-Gunner with the highest media profile, Ian Wright has commented on sport as well as presented television game shows and his own chat show. In April 2008, Wright criticised the BBC for their coverage of football. "Times are changing," he said. "I don't know how long young people are going to want to sit down and watch that same old 'jacket, shirt and tie format'. They want people who are dressed like them. They've got no one to relate to and that's why I've said to [the BBC] I don't want to do the England games any more. I feel like I'm just there as a comedy jester to break the ice with Alan Shearer and Alan Hansen who just do run-of-the-mill things."

George Graham, Alan Smith, Frank Stapleton and Frank McLintock, MBE have all worked as pundits on Sky Sports. Graham and Smith have both worked as co-commentators on Sky's live match coverage, while Stapleton and McLintock are regulars on Sky Sports News.

GOAL CRAZY ARSENAL

On Monday 5 December 1904, Woolwich Arsenal invited a team made up of footballers from various Parisian clubs to a game at the Manor Ground. A crowd of around 3,000 turned up to watch the spectacle which turned into something of a French farce – not helped by the French side having to borrow an Arsenal reserve player called Hodges to make up their team. The final score was rather emphatic: Woolwich Arsenal 26 Paris XI 1. *The Daily Express* reporter covering the match rather cruelly – although no doubt accurately – said, "Any one of our school XIs would easily have given the Paris team of yesterday a beating." The goals came from Watson (7), Ransom, Coleman (4), Briercliffe (4), Buchan (2), Linward (2), Hunter (5), and Blackman. The Woolwich Arsenal team was: Jimmy Ashcroft, Arthur Cross, Blackman, Jim Bigden, James Buchan, Frank Ransom, Tommy Briercliffe, John Hunter, Robert Watson, Tim Coleman, William Linward.

UP FOR THE CUP – XIII

Arsenal 3 Manchester United 2

Arsenal were back at Wembley for their second final in consecutive years and for their opponents were Manchester United, it was their third final in four years. On Saturday 12 May 1979 Arsenal were determined to make up for their defeat the year before to Ipswich Town. There were 15 internationals on the pitch but the game was hardly chockfull of skill and finesse. Arsenal had despatched assistant manager Wilf Dixon and ex-Gunner George Male to compile a dossier on United's weaknesses. They worked out that the United defence had a tendency to bunch together and did not defend the far post during crosses. Brian Talbot had subsequently signed for Arsenal from Ipswich Town for £450,000 and thus became the first and only player to have played in different FA Cup Final winning teams in successive seasons. He also opened Arsenal's account from a cross by David Price after a run by Liam Brady. In the Arsenal goal, Jennings was forced into making some good saves to keep the score 1-0. On 43 minutes, Liam Brady crossed and Frank Stapleton headed goal number two for Arsenal. Half time came and went and Arsenal seemed to be cruising to an easy win. Then Terry Neill made what is still to some a surprising substitution – he pulled off midfielder David Price and sent on defender Steve Walford. The decision upset the balance of the Arsenal side and suddenly Manchester United sniffed a chance. From a free kick Joe Jordan pulled the ball across Arsenal's goal for Gordon McQueen to score and then two minutes later, Sammy McIlroy made it 2-2. It seemed that extra time would be needed as with the 1971 game. Liam Brady said, "When United pulled level I was dreading extra time because I was knackered and our substitute was already on." He needn't have worried – he and Arsenal had other ideas: Brady spotted Graham Rix on the left side of the pitch and passed to him, Rix took off and crossed the ball. Gary Bailey in goal for United misjudged the cross and Alan Sunderland managed to connect with it with enough force to send it over the goal line and give Arsenal a last-minute victory. Arsenal: Pat Jennings, Pat Rice (captain), Sammy Nelson, Brian Talbot, David O'Leary, Willie Young, Liam Brady, Alan Sunderland, Frank Stapleton, David Price (Steve Walford), Graham Rix.

THE THINGS THEY SAY – XII

"I didn't watch the England-Argentina match in 1998. I can't remember why not. It may have been past my bedtime."

Theo Walcott, 2006

THE MAGIC SPONGE FOR CLUB AND COUNTRY

The following have been physios for Arsenal and England.

Tom Whittaker, MBE

Whittaker was trainer when England played Italy at the Battle of Highbury in November 1934.

Fred Street

Originally a physical training instructor in the RAF, Fred Street worked in London hospitals in the Fifties often with Bertie Mee, who had become Rehabilitation Officer at London's Camden Road Centre. In 1960, Mee became Arsenal physio and when he became manager in 1966, Street took over his old job at the Camden Road Centre. Eleven years later, in 1971, Arsenal coach Don Howe left Highbury for West Bromwich Albion taking physio George Wright with him. Mee rang Fred Street and asked him to come to Arsenal. For the next 13 years, Street's bald head was a regular sight at Highbury. He worked for England from 1974 until 1996.

Gary Lewin

Lewin left Arsenal on Thursday 31 July 2008 after new England boss Fabio Capello wanted a full-time physio in his England set-up. A bigger pay packet and the chance to ravel the world observing new techniques for coping with inuries provided too much of a lure for Lewin who had been with Arsenal since 1980 and first team physio since 1986 replacing Roy Johnson. He began working for England in 1996.

Billy Milne, DCM

After his career ended through injury, Billy Milne became Tom Whittaker's assistant at Highbury taking over the top job in July of 1947, a position he held until May 1960 (when Bertie Mee took over). He also was England trainer on many occasions.

FAIR PLAY TO ARSENAL

On Saturday 13 February 1999, Arsenal met Sheffield United in the fifth round of the FA Cup at Highbury. Patrick Vieira scored to put Arsenal one-up but Marcelo pulled one back for the Blades. In the 76th minute as United attacked, the ball was cleared but Lee Morris of United fell over in the Arsenal box stricken with cramp. The ball went to United goalie Alan Kelly who kicked it out of touch so that his team mate could get treatment. Morris went off and Bobby Ford came on as substitute. Ray Parlour took the throw-in for Arsenal and as is the convention threw it in the direction of the Sheffield United goal. Kanu in his first appearance for Arsenal was unaware of the tradition and trapped the ball before crossing to Marc Overmars who scored. The referee Peter Jones from Loughborough was left in a quandary – technically, the Arsenal players had nothing wrong but in the spirit of fair play they were wrong, albeit unknowingly. He awarded the goal. United players were understandably furious and their manager Steve Bruce threatened to get them to leave the pitch in protest. It was six minutes before the game could be restarted. At the final whistle, then vice-chairman David Dein and Arsène Wenger discussed the matter and decided to offer to replay the game. The FA agreed to Arsenal's suggestion but Fifa were reluctant fearing it could set a precedent. Finally, they agreed but insisted that both clubs sign a legally binding document stating that they agreed to abide by the result of the rearranged fixture and that part of the gate money must be donated to charity. The game was replayed and Arsenal won 2-1. Two clubs who had also been involved in a similar incident (both against Arsenal) but had not been as fair as the Gunners were Spurs (on Sunday 24 November 1996) and Blackburn Rovers (on Saturday 19 April 1997).

UP FOR THE CUP – XIV

Arsenal 0 West Ham United 1

Three years, three FA Cup Finals – Arsenal looked as if they were making Wembley a second home. On Saturday 10 May 1980 before 100,000 fans, they faced Second Division West Ham United. The Hammers won 1-0. Arsenal: Pat Jennings, Pat Rice (captain), John Devine (Sammy Nelson), Brian Talbot, David O'Leary, Willie Young, Liam Brady, Alan Sunderland, Frank Stapleton, David Price, Graham Rix.

BEST AND WORSE: WINS AND DEFEATS

Wins

Division One .... 9-1 v Grimsby Town (h)..................... 28 Jan 1931
Division Two .... 12-0 v Loughborough Town (h)..... 12 Mar 1900
Premier League .... 7-0 v Everton (h) .... 12 May 2005
.... 7-0 v Middlesbrough (h) .... 14 Jan 2006
FA Cup .... 12-0 v Ashford United (h)............... 14 Oct 1893
League Cup .... 7-0 v Leeds United (h)........................ 4 Sep 1979
European Cup............. 6-1 v FK Austria (h)............................... Sep 1991
Cup Winners' Cup...... 7-0 v Standard Liege (a) ....3 Nov 1993
Uefa Cup..................... 4-1 v Lokomotiv Leipzig (a).............27 Sep 1978
Champions League..... 7-0 v Slavia Prague (h) .... 23 Oct 2007

Defeats

Division One .... 0-7 v Blackburn Rovers (a)...................2 Oct 1909
.... 0-7 v West Bromwich Albion (a).......14 Oct 1922
.... 0-7 v Newcastle United (a)...................3 Oct 1925
.... 0-7 v West Ham United (a) ....7 Mar 1927
Division Two .... 0-8 v Loughborough Town (a) ....12 Dec 1896
Premier League .... 1-6 v Manchester United (a).............25 Feb 2001
FA Cup .... 0-6 v Derby County (h)...................... 28 Jan 1899
League Cup .... 0-5 v Chelsea (h) .... 11 Nov 1999
European Cup............. 1-3 v Benfica (h)....................................6 Nov 1991
Cup Winners' Cup...... 4-5 v Valencia (neutral) *on penalties*.. 14 May 1980
Uefa Cup..................... 2-5 v Spartak Moscow (h)................. 29 Sep 1982
Champions League..... 1-4 v Spartak Moscow (a) ....22 Nov 2000

UP FOR THE CUP – XV

Arsenal 0 Valencia 0 (4-5 on penalties)

Four days after the loss to West Ham United in the FA Cup Final, another cup final for the Gunners. Sadly another defeat as they went down on 5-4 penalties to Valencia in the European Cup Winners' Cup Final before 40,000 fans on Wednesday 14 May 1980 at Heysel Stadium in Brussels, Belgium. Arsenal: Pat Jennings, Pat Rice (captain), Sammy Nelson, Brian Talbot, David O'Leary, Willie Young, Liam Brady, Alan Sunderland, Frank Stapleton, David Price (John Hollins), Graham Rix.

ARSENAL FILMS

The Arsenal Stadium Mystery

Made in 1939, the film is set against the background of a match between Arsenal and The Trojans (played by Brentford in a special kit for the occasion). One of the opposition players drops dead during the match and it is revealed that he has been murdered. But whodunit? His team mates? His ex-girlfriend? Detective Inspector Slade (Leslie Banks) arrives to solve the case. Gunners manager George Allison has a speaking part including the immortal line "One-nil to the Arsenal and that's how we like it" and the rest of the team appear. The match footage was shot on 6 May 1939 during the First Division game – it was the last match of the 1938-39 season and Arsenal's last official league fixture before the outbreak of the Second World War. The film was released on 17 February 1940.

Fever Pitch

Published in 1992, Nick Hornby's autobiographical work won the William Hill Sports Book of the Year. Five years later, it was made into a film released on Friday 4 April 1997 and starring Colin Firth as English teacher Paul Ashworth and Ruth Gemmell as his girlfriend Sarah Hughes. The film's advertising tagline was: "Life gets complicated when you love one woman and worship eleven men". The final scenes for the film, set around the time of Arsenal's Championship-winning match at Anfield, were shot outside Highbury. Nick Hornby has a cameo role as an Arsenal supporter in the background of one scene. By the time the film came to be made Highbury's terracing had changed so the footage of fans on the terraces was shot at Fulham's Craven Cottage. In 2005 an American version of the film was made starring Drew Barrymore and Jimmy Fallon who is in love with the Boston Red Sox.

LE PROF SPEAKS – I

"At some clubs success is accidental. At Arsenal it is compulsory."
On his first double as manager, 1998.

"Having Ruddock claiming to be a nice guy was shocking, Some people behave like monsters and the next day they ay they're not guilty."
Defending Patrick Vieira, who was fined for spitting at Neil Ruddock, 1999.

PLAYED FOR BOTH ARSENAL & SPURS

Charles Ambler

Goalie Ambler made only two first-team appearances for the Gunners after signing professional terms for the club in July 1893. In October 1894, he signed for Spurs and the following year rejoined Arsenal. In September 1901, he moved to West Ham United.

David Bentley

Bentley signed for Arsenal when he was 13 and made his debut for the first team in the 2-0 FA Cup win against Oxford United in January 2003. Loaned to Norwich City he returned to Arsenal in 2005, but made only one appearance before joining Blackburn Rovers in January 2006. He joined Spurs for £15million on 31 July 2008 with Arsenal benefiting financially from the deal that saw him go to Ewood Park.

Jimmy Brain

A forward and former Welsh miner, Jimmy Brain signed for Arsenal in August 1923 and made his First Division debut against Tottenham Hotspur at Highbury on 25 October 1924 when he scored and Arsenal won 1–0. In September 1931 after more than 200 first-team appearances and 125 goals, Brain signed for Spurs where he stayed for four years, including two as player-coach. Realising his folly, when he retired he returned home to become an Arsenal scout.

Stan Briggs

Briggs never signed pro with any of his teams. He played for Tottenham FC and Tottenham Hotspur. In October 1893, he joined Arsenal but stayed for just a month making two league appearances.

Laurie Brown

In 1960, Laurie Brown represented Great Britain in the Rome Olympics and won 14 amateur caps for England as a centre-forward. In August 1961 he joined Arsenal from Northampton Town for £10,000. He made his debut against Burnley on 19 August 1961 in a 2-2 draw at Highbury. Arsenal converted him into a fine centre-half and he played more than 100 games before leaving for Spurs in February 1964 for a fee of £40,000. His first match for Spurs was against Arsenal and Spurs won 3-1.

Lycurgus Burrows

Of all the players in this book, Ly Burrows is unique in not only having played for Woolwich Arsenal and Spurs but having played for Woolwich Arsenal twice and Spurs three times. In January 1892, full-back Burrows signed for Woolwich Arsenal as an amateur. He made his debut on 6 February 1894 against Rotherham Town. When Joe Powell joined the club Burrows found his chances of first-team football waning and in October 1894 he signed for Spurs. He played more than 60 times for Woolwich Arsenal's deadly rivals before returning to Arsenal in October 1895 where he played just one game against Notts County before returning to Tottenham Marshes for two years. He joined Sheffield United in December 1897 but by March 1898 was back at Northumberland Park, Spurs's then home ground after leaving Tottenham Marshes.

James Caldwell

Goalie who crossed the divide 65 years before Pat Jennings. Jim Caldwell signed for Spurs in August 1908 but stayed just two months before joining Reading. In June 1913, he moved to Woolwich Arsenal (from Everton) but struggled to win a place in the team and after just three league appearances was on the move (back to Reading in July 1914). The First World War forced his retirement.

Sol Campbell

Of all the players who have played for both clubs, Sol Campbell has probably received more stick than any other. Cries of "Judas" and "Traitor" have echoed around Tottenham when he returned to the club he served so loyally but clad in Arsenal's red and white. He began his career at White Hart Lane in 1990 and spent almost 11 years with Spurs making more than 300 first team appearances before a shock free transfer under the Bosman ruling saw him move to Highbury. During his time with Spurs they had never finished higher than seventh and Campbell had expressed a wish to actually win something at club level. In his first season at Highbury, Campbell won championship and FA Cup winner's medals as Arsenal completed the double. In May 2006, Campbell scored the first goal in the Champions League Final against Barcelona at the Stade de France, Paris, after goalie Jens Lehmann had been sent off for a professional foul. The Spaniards upped their game and beat ten-man Arsenal 2-1. On Saturday 8 July 2006, Arsenal announced that Campbell had left the club.

Freddie Cox

Freddie Cox, an outside right, joined Spurs in July 1938 as an amateur. In September 1949, Arsenal paid £12,000 to obtain his services, In four years at Highbury he played in two FA Cup Finals (one was won and one lost) and won a League Championship medal in 1953.

James Devlin

Dundee-born Devlin signed for Spurs in August 1896 from Airdrieonians. In December 1897 Woolwich Arsenal paid £80 to Sunderland to sign him and he made his debut on New Year's Day 1898 scoring in a 3-3 draw at Blackpool. Unfortunately, while he contracted pleurisy and in August 1898 went back to Airdrieonians as he was swapped for John Dick.

Arthur Elliott

Inside-left Arthur Elliott signed for Arsenal in July 1892. He scored on his league debut, Woolwich Arsenal's first Second Division match, against Newcastle United on 2 September 1893. He played two dozen times for Arsenal in the league scoring 11 goals and ten times in the FA Cup scoring nine times. In August 1894, he moved to Spurs.

Tom Fitchie

Amateur Tom Fitchie joined Woolwich Arsenal in November 1901 from Queens Park Rangers but the next month joined Spurs. In February 1902, he was back at the Arsenal where he stayed for four years. He was back for this third and final time at Woolwich Arsenal in September 1908. He played 56 league games and scored 27 goals for Woolwich Arsenal.

Vic Groves

He signed with Spurs as an amateur in 1952 and made four appearances before moving on to Walthamstow Avenue. A move to Leyton Orient followed but he did not hit his stride until his move to Highbury in November 1955. He played more than 200 games for the Gunners scoring almost 40 goals as well as wearing the captain's armband on occasion.

Tom Hatfield

Goalkeeper who joined Woolwich Arsenal in January 1895 but was limited to just two league appearances before signing for Spurs in June 1896. He made ten appearances for Spurs.

George Hunt

Hunt joined Spurs in June 1930 and scored 138 goals in 198 games. Three years later, he was capped for England. In October 1937, he joined Arsenal as a replacement for Ted Drake and Hunt made his debut against Manchester City on 2 October 1937 at Highbury. Hunt never settled at Arsenal and was sold to Bolton Wanderers in the summer of 1938.

David Jenkins

An apprentice with Arsenal in June 1962, Jenkins signed professional terms in October 1963. His opportunities were limited at Highbury although he did play in the 1968 League Cup Final against Leeds United. In October 1968, he was part of a £50,000 exchange deal that took him to White Hart Lane and Jimmy Robertson to Highbury. He spent three and a half years at Tottenham.

Pat Jennings, MBE, OBE

Many Spurs fans are to this day mystified why goalkeeping legend Jennings was allowed to leave White Hart Lane at all, never mind being allowed to sign for Arsenal. After 13 years, an FA Cup winner's medal, two League Cup winner's medals and a Uefa Cup winner's medal in his trophy cabinet, Jennings moved across north London in August 1977. The move gave him a new lease of life and he displaced first-choice keeper Jimmy Rimmer, three years his junior. Jennings made his debut for Arsenal against Ipswich Town on 20 August 1977 (although he let in a goal and the Gunners lost 1-0). He was a regular between the sticks for the next seven years, making his last appearance against Sheffield Wednesday on 25 November 1984. Again, Arsenal lost – this time 2-1. Jennings made 327 appearances for Arsenal, 237 of them in the First Division. In July 1985, Arsenal gave Jennings a free transfer and Spurs re-signed him.

John Julian

Julian signed for Woolwich Arsenal in July 1889 but continued working in the armaments factory. In September 1894, he moved to Spurs.

Leonard Julians

Born in Tottenham, he signed for Spurs in 1954 before moving to Leyton Orient. In December 1958, Arsenal paid the Os £12,000 for his services. He spent most of his time in the reserves and left in May 1960.

Peter Kyle

Forward Kyle joined Spurs in late May 1905 but stayed at Tottenham for only a short time before signing for Woolwich Arsenal in April 1906. He played 52 league games for the Gunners and scored 21 goals before leaving for Aston Villa in March 1908.

Billy Milne, DCM

Milne spent two weeks with Spurs on a trial basis before he saw the light and moved to Highbury where he would spend much of the next 39 years as player and then trainer.

Rohan Ricketts

Clapham-born midfielder Ricketts signed for Arsenal on Wednesday 1 August 2001 but played just once in the League Cup, against Manchester United. Realising his opportunities at Highbury were limited he signed for Spurs on Saturday 13 July 2002. He shone under Glenn Hoddle at Spurs but failed to make an impression on Martin Jol and moved to Wolves on Monday 14 March 2005. On 11 April 2008, after a spell at QPR and Barnsley, he signed for Toronto in Canada.

Jimmy Robertson

He joined Spurs in March 1964 and played 177 times for the club and scored 31 goals before he joined Arsenal in October 1968 in a £55,000 deal that saw David Jenkins going the opposite way to White Hart Lane. Robertson spent 18 months at Highbury and displaced John Radford from the inside-right position resulting in Radford moving to centre-forward. Robertson stayed at Arsenal for a little under 18 months before joining Ipswich Town because Bertie Mee preferred George Armstrong.

Kevin Stead

Stead joined Spurs in April 1974 but failed to make the first team before he was given a free transfer to Arsenal in July 1977. In two years at Arsenal, he only made two appearances (one as substitute).

Andrew Swann

Scottish-born centre-forward Swann joined Woolwich Arsenal in May 1901 and made seven appearances for the first team. In May 1904, he joined Spurs where he stayed for ten months.

Steve Walford

Steve Walford joined Spurs in 1974 but managed only two games in the first team before he joined Arsenal in August 1977, Terry Neill paying £25,000 for his services. A useful centre-back, Walford was more of a regular utility player rather than a first choice. Nevertheless, he played 64 times for Arsenal in the First Division with another 13 as substitute. His last appearance in an Arsenal shirt came in a 2–2 draw against Middlesbrough on 28 February 1981. In March 1981, he moved to Norwich City for £175,000 (Willie Young would also play for Arsenal, Spurs and Norwich.)

Charlie Williams

He joined Woolwich Arsenal in November 1891 and kept goal in the first match played in the football league on Saturday 2 September 1893 against Newcastle United at the Manor Ground, Plumstead. He spent two and a half years with the club before he moved on to Manchester City in June 1894. On 14 April 1900, while playing for City against Sunderland at Roker Park, he became the first goalkeeper in league history to score a goal, with a long clearance. From City, he moved to Spurs where he stayed for 11 months. In 1908, he was coach of the Danish Olympic side that won the silver medal. In 1912, he got a job with a Brazilian team and stayed there for the rest of his life. He died at Rio de Janeiro in 1952.

Willie Young

The red-headed Scotsman joined Spurs in September 1975 but never made much of an impression with the fans at White Hart Lane. He did make an impression on Terry Neill however, because the Irishman signed him for a second time, bringing him to Highbury in March 1977 for £80,000. He made his debut against Ipswich Town on 5 March at Highbury. The Tractor Boys ran out 4-1 winners. Terry Neill commented, "He tried to play like Pele, George Best and Gerson rolled into one. He should have remembered that he was a 14-stone Scotsman." It took a while for the North Bank to accept Young – they were never sure whether he was going to make a brilliant tackle or hoick the ball into the upper tier of the West Stand – but he eventually became a firm favourite. In 1980, he caused controversy when he scythed down Paul Allen in the FA Cup Final. After more than 230 games, Young joined Nottingham Forest in December 1981 for £50,000.

CHAIRMEN OF THE BOARD

Until 1912..George Leavey
1912-1929 .... Sir Henry Norris
1929-1936 .... Sir Samuel Hill-Wood
1936 .... 5th Earl of Lonsdale
1936-1939 ....8th Earl of Granard
1939-1946 .... 8th Marquess of Londonderry, Viscount Castlereagh
1946-1949 .... Sir Samuel Hill-Wood
1949-1962 ....Sir Bracewell Smith
1962-1982 .... Denis Hill-Wood
1982-..Peter Hill-Wood

SPURS TO ARSENAL - ARSENAL TO SPURS

Herbert Chapman

The man who modernised football as well as Arsenal joined Spurs as a player in 1905 for £75. In his first season, he scored 11 goals but in the second season, he was unable to maintain his place in the team and netted just three times. At the end of the season, Chapman retired from playing.

Joe Hulme

After almost 12 years at Highbury, Joe Hulme joined Huddersfield for £500 in January 1938. His last appearance for the club was against Liverpool on 18 December 1937. In 1944, Hulme began work at White Hart Lane and in October 1945, he became manager of Spurs, a job he held until May 1949.

UP FOR THE CUP – XVI

Arsenal 2 Liverpool 1

Finally, Arsenal won the one domestic trophy that eluded them for so long – the League Cup. Ninety-six thousand people at Wembley watched as Charlie Nicholas scored both goals as Arsenal beat Liverpool 2-1 on 5 April 1987. Arsenal: John Lukic, Viv Anderson, Kenny Sansom (captain), Steve Williams, David O'Leary, Tony Adams, David Rocastle, Paul Davis, Niall Quinn (Perry Groves), Charlie Nicholas, Martin Hayes (Michael Thomas)

ARSENAL CELEBRATE WINNING THE 1987 LEAGUE CUP

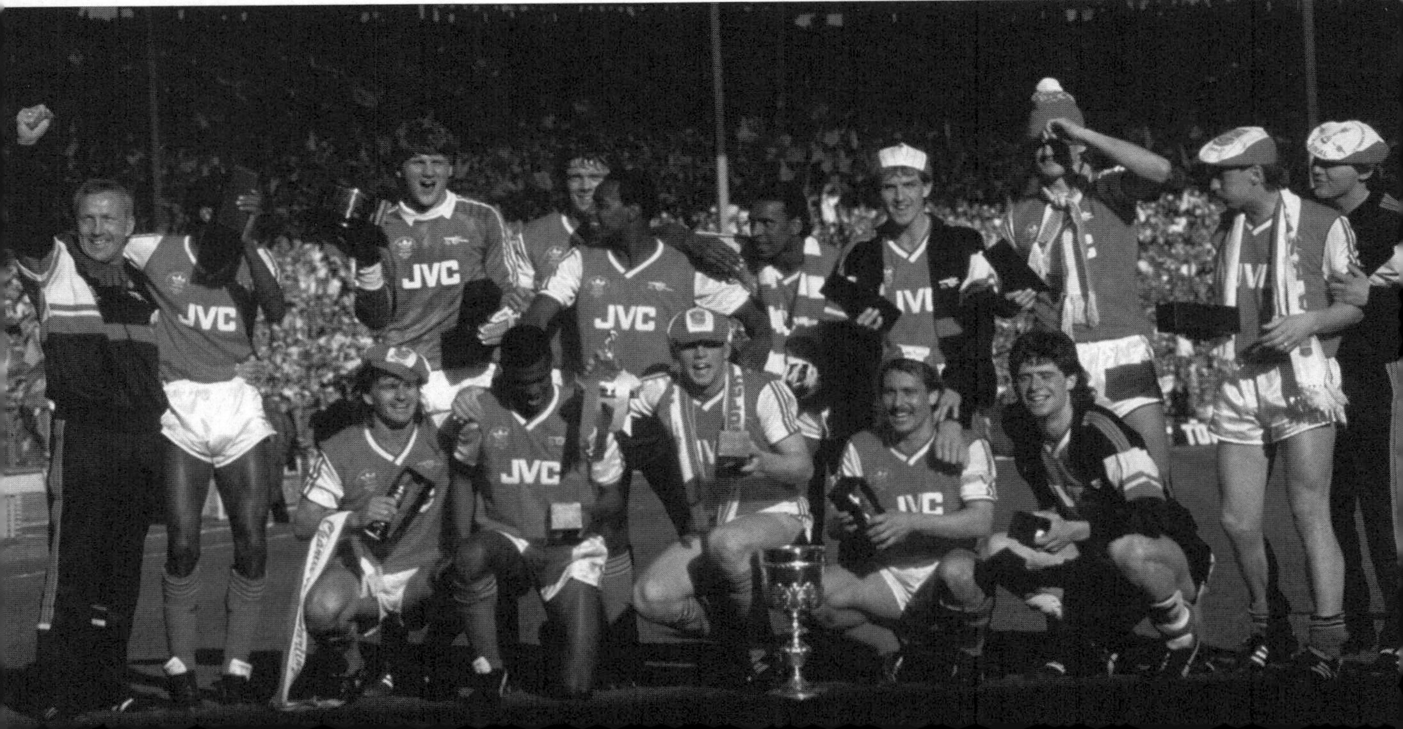

GROUND BY GROUND

1887-1888 The Sportsman Ground, Plumstead Marshes, Kent

A former venue for breeding pigs, the first home ground was rented for matches. The club left the Sportsman when the ground flooded.

1888-1890, 1893-1913 Manor Ground, Plumstead Marshes, Kent

In 1888, Royal Arsenal moved next door to the Manor Ground, then known as Manor Field, where they stayed for two years. The club's first match there was a 3-3 draw against Millwall Rovers, on 11 February 1888. The pitch was nearly always muddy and behind the south goal was an open sewer. Club secretary Elijah Watkins commented that play often had to be stopped while "mud" was wiped off the ball. There were no stands and the club borrowed wagons from the Army for spectators to sit in. After a financial disagreement with the owner of the Invicta Ground, Woolwich Arsenal returned to the Manor Ground where they stayed for 20 years. A share issue raised the necessary funds to buy the ground and there was enough money to build a stand and banks of terraces. In January 1895, there was crowd trouble during a match against Burton Wanderers and the Football League ordered that the Manor Ground be closed for five weeks. Woolwich Arsenal played a game each at New Brompton's Priestfield Stadium (against Burton Swifts) and at Lyttelton cricket ground, Leyton (against Leicester Fosse). In 1904, the club built a second stand, it was the first to be nicknamed the Spion Kop. At first, attendances at the Manor Ground were around 20,000 but they began to drop not least because of the isolation of the venue in an industrial area. In 1910, with Woolwich Arsenal facing bankruptcy, London property magnate and Fulham chairman Sir Henry Norris bought the club. His first plan was to merge the two clubs but the Football League refused him permission. Norris was a man of foresight not to mention deviousness and he realised that Woolwich Arsenal could not flourish in Woolwich and moved the club to north London to a new home at Highbury. Woolwich Arsenal played their last match at the Manor Ground on Saturday 26 April 1913, a 1-1 draw with Middlesbrough watched by just 3,000 people. Once the venue was no longer home to football, the ground became derelict. It was later demolished and redeveloped. Today it is an industrial estate once more. The Manor Ground was on land that's now Nathan Way, Griffin Manor Way and Hadden Road.

1890-1893 Invicta Ground, Plumstead High Street South, Kent

In 1890, Royal Arsenal moved to the more salubrious surroundings of the Invicta Ground – it had changing rooms, a stand and terraces. In 1891 the club was renamed Woolwich Arsenal and turned professional. They returned to the Manor Ground when the owner of the Invicta Ground, George Weaver, owner of the Weaver Mineral Water Company, raised the rent from £200 to £350. He had hoped to cash in on the club's success but they called his bluff and went back to their old home. An amateur team, Royal Ordnance Factories, moved into the Invicta Ground for a short period but they left in 1894 and Weaver could not find new tenants. He knocked down the ground and developed the land for houses. Today, Mineral Street and Hector Street stand where the stadium used to be. Some of its concrete terracing still survives in the back gardens of houses in Hector Street.

1913-2006 Arsenal Stadium, Avenell Road, Highbury, London

Arsenal Stadium, Highbury, "The Home of Football" – three names for the same place. A football ground next to a London Underground station in north London became an iconic sporting venue and an architectural one. Built in 1913 on the six-acre recreation fields belonging to St John's College of Divinity after they were leased for 21 years at a cost of £20,000, the stadium was designed by Archibald Leitch and cost £125,000 to be built. (Leitch had previously worked on Hampden Park, Ibrox, Parkhead and Goodison Park.) Local residents opposed the building of the stadium, as did representatives from Clapton Orient, Chelsea and Tottenham Hotspur who saw their gates decreasing in size and thus revenue. Sir Henry Norris overcame residents' objections by saying that 30,000 supporters every Saturday was not all that many and anyway they would be good for business. The local newspapers did not carry much in the way of protest because they had been silenced by Norris's contacts within the Fourth Estate. Norris promised that no matches would be played at the new ground on Christmas Day or Good Friday and that alcohol would not be served there. That remained in place until 1925. The first game played at the still uncompleted Arsenal Stadium was a Second Division match on Saturday 6 September 1913 against Leicester Fosse. Tommy Benfield of Leicester scored the very first goal at the new ground and George Jobey scored the first Arsenal goal as the Gunners ran out 2-1 winners.

Highbury played host to its first England match on Monday 15 March 1920 (England lost 2-1 to Wales). Three years later, on Monday 19 March 1923, Highbury was host to the first England match against foreign opposition – Belgium were the visitors and lost 6-1. In 1925, the club bought the stadium outright at a cost of £64,000. The college became a tenant of Arsenal until the Second World War when a fire destroyed the building. On Saturday 5 November 1932, Gillespie Road tube station was renamed Arsenal, the only station on the network named after a football club. The following month, on Saturday 10 December 1932, the Prince of Wales opened the art deco West Stand before a match against Chelsea. Designed by Claude Waterlow Ferrier and William Binnie, it cost £45,000. In October 1936, the East Stand was opened but it went over budget and cost £130,000. The North Bank (previously called the Laundry End) was covered, design also by Waterlow Ferrier. The large clock erected on the say-so of Herbert Chapman was moved to the other end giving rise to the name the Clock End. During the Second World War, the ground was a first aid post and air raid patrol centre and (whisper it) Arsenal played their games at White Hart Lane. The North Bank received a direct hit by a German bomber destroying the roof and it remained open to the elements until 1956. On Wednesday 17 October 1951, Arsenal played Hapoel Tel Aviv in the first match under floodlights at Highbury. In 1964, the club, always ahead of its time, installed undersoil heating at a cost of £15,000 which meant that games rarely had to be called off because of bad weather. When games were cancelled, it was usually due to the state of the terraces – the pitch was immaculate. Immaculate it may have been but the pitch was too small to host World Cup games when the tournament came to England in 1966. Following the publication of the Taylor Report in January 1990, Arsenal Stadium became an all-seater venue with a capacity reduced from 60,000 to 38,419, which did not generate enough revenue. The last game played there was on Sunday 7 May 2006 against Wigan Athletic. Arsenal won 4-2 with a hat-trick from Thierry Henry. That summer the bulldozers moved in to turn the stadium into Highbury Square, a series 711 of small and costly apartments with the pitch area becoming a communal garden. The East and West Stands have been preserved in the new development, which is expected to open in 2010. The development topped out on Thursday 6 March 2008.

2006- Emirates Stadium, Ashburton Grove, London

In the late-Nineties, it became apparent that Arsenal were outgrowing Highbury and began looking around for a new home. Then vice-chairman David Dein wanted the club to move to Wembley but this was met with opposition in many quarters and the plan was abandoned. A site was finally found at an industrial estate at Ashburton Grove, a long goalkeeper's kick away from Arsenal Stadium. In November 1999, the scheme to move Arsenal was announced and the scheduled opening date was August 2003. It became apparent that this was too optimistic and the finance was not in place so it was delayed until July 2006. Arsenal had to pay for the existing tenants at Ashburton Grove to relocate which added to the expense of the move. Construction of the stadium by Sir Robert McAlpine began in February 2004. The stadium topped out in August 2005, and was completed ahead of schedule and on budget. On Tuesday 5 October 2004, it was announced that the new venue would be known as the Emirates Stadium for at least 15 years after the airline agreed a £100million sponsorship deal with Arsenal. Beginning in 2006-07 the Emirates would also be the shirt sponsors for eight years. The stadium opened in July 2006 and the first match played there was Dennis Berkamp's testimonial against Ajax of Amsterdam. The ground is the biggest in London after Wembley and Twickenham, and the second biggest in the league after Old Trafford. The Duke of Edinburgh officially opened the Emirates Stadium on Thursday 26 October 2006. The Queen had also been due to attend but was hampered by a bad back. On 15 February 2007, she invited the directors, management and first team squad to a reception at Buckingham Palace – the first time a football team has been so honoured – leading to a belief that Her Majesty is a Gooner.

UP FOR THE CUP – XVII

Arsenal 2 Luton Town 3

Arsenal returned to Wembley to defend the League Cup on Sunday 24 April 1988 where they met Luton Town. Despite goals from Martin Hayes and Alan Smith, 95,732 spectators saw Luton win 3-2. Arsenal: John Lukic, Nigel Winterburn, Kenny Sansom, Michael Thomas, Gus Caesar, Tony Adams (captain), David Rocastle, Paul Davis, Alan Smith, Perry Groves (Martin Hayes), Kevin Richardson.

THE ARSENAL – DECADE BY DECADE: 1940s

1946-47

First Division	P	W	D	L	F	A	W	D	L	F	A	Pts
13. Arsenal	42	9	5	7	43	33	7	4	10	29	37	41

FA Cup: Third round

1947-48

First Division	P	W	D	L	F	A	W	D	L	F	A	Pts
1. Arsenal	42	15	3	3	56	15	8	10	3	25	17	59

FA Cup: Third round

1948-49

First Division	P	W	D	L	F	A	W	D	L	F	A	Pts
5. Arsenal	42	13	5	3	51	18	5	8	8	23	26	49

FA Cup: Fourth round

1949-50

First Division	P	W	D	L	F	A	W	D	L	F	A	Pts
6. Arsenal	42	12	4	5	48	24	7	7	7	31	31	49

FA Cup: Winners

1939-1945 the Football League was suspended due to the Second World War.

CROWD PLEASERS

On Saturday 9 March 1935, Highbury welcomed its biggest ever attendance when 73,295 turned up to watch a First Division match against Sunderland. The match ended 0-0. The biggest attendance at the Emirates (so far) was 60,132 against Reading on Saturday 3 March 2007. When Arsenal played their European matches at Wembley, the biggest attendance was 73,707 against RC Lens on Wednesday 25 November 1998. The lowest attendances for Arsenal matches have been 4,554 in the First Division against Leeds United on Thursday 5 May 1966 (the Gunners lost 3-0) and 18,253 against Wimbledon in the Premier League on Wednesday 10 February 1993. The lowest Wembley attendance for a European game was 71,227 in the match against AIK Solna on Wednesday 22 September 1999.

SKIN OF THE TEETH STUFF

On Friday 1 May 1953, Arsenal needed to beat Burnley for their seventh League Championship. The match began with a flurry of attacks for Arsenal but Burnley counterattacked and Roy Stephenson put them ahead. Arsenal responded and within 11 minutes were 3-1 ahead thanks to goals from Alex Forbes, Doug Lishman and Jimmy Logie. Billy Elliott to pull one back for the Clarets, and Burnley pushed forward for an equaliser but Arsenal pulled everyone back into defence. It was too much for Tom Whittaker who retired to the dressing room. He stayed there until the players returned to tell him that they had won. Champions Arsenal's goal average was 1.51; second place Preston North End's was 1.41.

AND THE AWARD GOES TO...

The Football Writers' Association Footballer of the Year was first presented in 1947–48. An Arsenal player has won it on seven occasions.

1949–50	Joe Mercer
1970–71	Frank McLintock
1997–98	Dennis Bergkamp
2001–02	Robert Pirès
2002–03, 2003–04, 2005–06	Thierry Henry

The PFA Players' Player of the Year was first presented in 1973–74. An Arsenal player has won it four times.

1978–79	Liam Brady
1997–98	Dennis Bergkamp
2002–03, 2003–04	Thierry Henry

The PFA Young Player of the Year (given to a player under 23) was first presented in 1973–74. An Arsenal player has won it on four occasions.

1986–87	Tony Adams
1988–89	Paul Merson
1998–99	Nicolas Anelka
2007–08	Francesc Fàbregas

UP FOR THE CUP – XVIII

Arsenal 2 Sheffield Wednesday 1

In 1992-93, Arsenal created history by becoming the first team to win both domestic cup competitions in the same season. In addition, oddly, their opponents in both finals were Sheffield Wednesday and on both occasions, the Gunners won 2-1. The first, the League Cup, was on Sunday 18 April 1993 at Wembley before 74,007 fans. Arsenal's goals came from Paul Merson and Steve Morrow (his first for the club) although 22-year-old Morrow was unable to enjoy most of the post-match celebrations. At the final whistle captain Tony Adams had picked Morrow up and promptly dropped him breaking his arm in the process. The match was the first in which any European clubs had used squad numbers instead of the usual one to eleven. Arsenal: David Seaman, David O'Leary, Nigel Winterburn, Paul Davis, Tony Adams (captain), Andy Linighan, Steve Morrow, Ray Parlour, Paul Merson, Ian Wright, Kevin Campbell.

THE ARSENAL – DECADE BY DECADE: 1950s

1950-51

First Division	P	W	D	L	F	A	W	D	L	F	A	Pts
5. Arsenal	42	11	5	5	47	28	8	4	9	26	28	47

FA Cup: Fifth round

1951-52

First Division	P	W	D	L	F	A	W	D	L	F	A	Pts
3. Arsenal	42	13	7	1	54	30	8	4	9	26	31	53

FA Cup: Runners-up

1952-53

First Division	P	W	D	L	F	A	W	D	L	F	A	Pts
1. Arsenal	42	15	3	3	60	30	6	9	6	37	34	54

FA Cup: Fifth round

1953-54

First Division	P	W	D	L	F	A	W	D	L	F	A	Pts
12. Arsenal	42	8	8	5	42	37	7	5	9	33	36	43

FA Cup: Fourth round

1954-55

First Division	P	W	D	L	F	A	W	D	L	F	A	Pts
9. Arsenal	42	12	3	6	44	25	5	6	10	25	38	43

FA Cup: Fourth round

1955-56

First Division	P	W	D	L	F	A	W	D	L	F	A	Pts
5. Arsenal	42	13	4	4	38	22	5	6	10	22	39	46

FA Cup: Sixth round

1956-57

First Division	P	W	D	L	F	A	W	D	L	F	A	Pts
5. Arsenal	42	12	5	4	45	21	9	3	9	40	48	50

FA Cup: Sixth round

1957-58

First Division	P	W	D	L	F	A	W	D	L	F	A	Pts
12. Arsenal	42	10	4	7	48	39	6	3	12	25	46	39

FA Cup: Third round

1958-59

First Division	P	W	D	L	F	A	W	D	L	F	A	Pts
3. Arsena;	42	14	3	4	53	29	7	5	9	35	39	50

FA Cup: Fifth round

1959-60

First Division	P	W	D	L	F	A	W	D	L	F	A	Pts
13. Arsenal	42	9	5	7	39	38	6	4	11	29	42	39

FA Cup: Third round

LE PROF SPEAKS – II

"I'm amazed how big Patrick's elbows are. They can reach players ten yards away. Let's just give him a 15-game ban and get it over and done with."
On Patrick Vieira, 2002

"We give people what they like to see – pace, commitment, attacking football – and sometimes if we go overboard, I'm sorry."
Trying to explain why the club had so many red cards, 2002

PLAYING POLITICS

After retirement footballers have a variety of options open to them but politics is not usually one of them. In September 1946, Arsenal signed Albert Gudmundsson, an Icelandic inside-forward. Unfortunately, he was unable to get a work permit and, after just two games for the Gunners, joined Inter Milan. On hanging up his boots, he became a successful businessman before his appointment as finance minister in the Icelandic government in 1983. Two years later, in 1985, he became minister of industry, until he resigned in 1987 following a tax scandal. He formed his own right-of-centre political party and in the 1987 elections received 10.9 per cent of the vote. He died on 7 April 1994, aged 70.

PLAYED FOR ARSENAL ON TWO OCCASIONS

Charles Ambler

Goalkeeper Ambler signed amateur terms for Woolwich Arsenal in August 1891 from Borstal Rovers. He spent one season with Arsenal before leaving in August 1892 to join Clapton to "gain experience". In July 1893, he rejoined Woolwich Arsenal as a pro but appeared in only two first-team matches, but he played 65 times for Arsenal at all levels.

Ted Batcup

A former Guardsman, Batcup joined Woolwich Arsenal in April 1905 turning professional the following month. He made his first team debut on 7 April 1906 against Manchester City when Woolwich Arsenal won 2-1. However, the brilliance of Jimmy Ashcroft kept him out of the side for much of the three years he spent at the club. In July 1908, Batcup moved to New Brompton but the lure of the Manor Ground was too much and in July 1910, he re-signed for Woolwich Arsenal.

Pat Beasley

In May 1931 Beasley, who played outside left, joined Arsenal from Stourbridge after Herbert Chapman paid £550. He won championship medals with the Gunners in 1934 and 1935. In October 1936, he was sold for £750, ironically to Chapman's old club Huddersfield Town. He returned to Arsenal as a guest player in 1940-41, 1941-42 and October-November 1945.

Frank Boulton

Goalkeeper Boulton signed for Arsenal in October 1936 from Bath City. He won a First Division Championship medal with the club in 1938 replacing George Swindin between the sticks. However, when Swindin regained his form, Boulton was relegated to the reserves and in August 1938, with Alex Wilson and George Marks also fighting for the number one jersey, he signed for Derby County. Boulton returned to Arsenal in the 1940-41 wartime season making another ten appearances.

Charles Buchan

Renaissance man Charlie Buchan joined Woolwich Arsenal as an amateur in December 1908 and played four times but left the club after their secretary–manager George Morrell refused to pay the 11 shillings expenses, which Buchan claimed as the cost of travelling to training and away games. He joined Northfleet for the rest of the season. Letting Buchan go was an error of judgment that was to have severe repercussions for the club. In July 1925, he rejoined Arsenal in a deal that was ultimately to bring about the downfall of club owner Sir Henry Norris (see page 172). At Arsenal Buchan became club captain and won a runners'-up medal in the 1927 FA Cup Final against Cardiff City. Buchan retired from football in 1928, his last game for Arsenal being the one in which Dixie Dean scored his record 60th goal of the season.

Jack Caldwell

Born in Shawwood, Ayrshire, left-back Caldwell joined Woolwich Arsenal from Hibernian in August 1894 and was ever present in the first team that 1894-95 season and missed only one game the following season before he lost his place to Finlay Sinclair. He signed for Third Lanark in August 1896 but missed Woolwich Arsenal so much he was back in October of the same year. He played a further 40 or so games for the Arsenal before finally leaving for Brighton United.

Ted Carr

A centre-forward, he signed with Arsenal as an amateur in February 1935 but the next month left for Margate to gain experience. He signed pro terms with Arsenal in August 1937. He scored seven goals in 12 games before injury and the Second World ended his Arsenal career.

Hugh Duff

In August 1895, Duff, an outside-left, joined Woolwich Arsenal as an amateur from Millwall Athletic but he did not make his first-team debut until 12 December 1896 in an FA Cup game against Leyton, due to bizarre circumstances. In modern times Arsène Wenger has often played what it effectively a second string side in the League Cup. On 12 December 1896 Arsenal had to play a league match on the same day as the cup tie, so they fielded a reserve side for the FA Cup and the first team for the league. The league side went down to their heaviest-ever defeat while the reserves smashed Leyton 5-0, with Duff on target! It was not until 4 December 1897 that he eventually made a league appearance for Arsenal, against Leicester Fosse. Just as he had on his first FA Cup appearance, he also scored on his Football League debut. In August 1898, he signed for Millwall but in July 1899, he returned to Woolwich Arsenal where he stayed until April 1900 but did not make an appearance in the first team.

Alf Fields, BEM

In January 1936, Fields signed for Arsenal but left for Margate the following month. He returned to Highbury in May 1937 and stayed for 10 years until an injury to ligaments in his left knee forced his retirement. Fields was crocked after colliding with George Swindin, his own goalie, in September 1947.

John Graham

He joined in December 1897 but left for Millwall Athletic four months later. Graham returned to Woolwich Arsenal in September 1899 but only managed to make the first team on one occasion (against Gainsborough Trinity on 14 October 1899 when Woolwich Arsenal won 2-1) during both spells.

Fred Groves

He signed for Woolwich Arsenal in October 1912 turning professional a year later. Seven years later, he joined Brighton & Hove Albion for £500. Five months and £150 later he was back at Woolwich Arsenal. Bizarrely, in March 1921 he rejoined Brighton & Hove Albion. He made most of his appearances in an Arsenal shirt during the First World War.

Bill Harper

In November 1925, Arsenal paid what was then the record fee of £4,500 for a goalkeeper when Bill Harper joined from Hibernian. He made his Arsenal debut against Bury on 14 November 1925 in a game that Arsenal won 6-1. He stayed at the club for 19 months before joining Fall River Marksman in Massachusetts, America. Three years later, after playing for various American teams he returned to Arsenal. He made more than 70 appearances between the posts for the Gunners – his last away to Blackburn Rovers on 31 August 1931 – before he moved to what was to become his second home Plymouth Argyle where he stayed for 54 years in various roles.

Joe Heath

In June 1893, Heath signed for Woolwich Arsenal from Wolverhampton Wanderers and on 11 September scored the club's first hat-trick in the league (against Walsall Town Swifts). In 1894-95, he was appointed player-reserve team coach. At the beginning of the 1895-96 season, he signed for Gravesend United. In January 1896, he returned to Woolwich Arsenal but languished in the reserves until he left in April 1897.

Martin Keown

Keown joined Arsenal on a schoolboy contract in October 1980 and became an apprentice in June 1982. He turned professional on 2 February 1984 and for the 1984-85 season, he was loaned to Brighton & Hove Albion where he made his league debut on 23 November 1985. Back at Arsenal, he made 22 appearances before he fell out with George Graham after asking for another £50 a week. On 9 June 1986, Graham sold Keown to Aston Villa for £125,000. The player spent three years there before moving to Everton on 7 August 1989. On Thursday 4 February 1993, Graham swallowed his pride and paid £2·2million to re-sign Keown from Goodison Park. Keown made 283 league appearances for Arsenal vying for the central defender's position with Steve Bould and Tony Adams. Keown remained at Arsenal until Tuesday 20 July 2004, before being released on a free transfer. He joined Leicester City. He played more than 450 games for the Arsenal and his dedication to the club could never be questioned. During one match, he is said to have yelled at a teammate, "Play like you want to play for the Arsenal."

John Lukic

John Lukic was born in Chesterfield and joined Arsenal in July 1983, for £75,000 from Leeds United. He replaced Pat Jennings in the Arsenal goal becoming a popular figure with the crowd. In 1990, George Graham paid £1.3m (a then British record for a keeper) to buy David Seaman, Lukic's deputy at Leeds. Lukic returned to Elland Road having played over 250 games for Arsenal. This time the fee was £1million. In 1996, he re-signed for Arsenal as cover for Seaman and was on the bench for the 2000 Uefa Cup Final when Arsenal lost to Galatasaray. On 17 October 2000, he became the then-oldest player to play in the Champions League.

Charlie McGibbon

He joined Woolwich Arsenal in August 1905 when he was a sergeant in the Royal Artillery but did not stay long. He returned in 1910 and made his debut against Chelsea on 28 March 1910, scoring the only goal.

David Neave

An outside-left, Neave joined Woolwich Arsenal in March 1904 but spent much of his time in the reserves. He departed for Leyton Orient but in December 1905 was back and made more than 150 appearances.

Gordon Nutt

He joined Arsenal as an amateur in 1946 but was not thought up to the appropriate standard and he was released. Nine years later, he returned to Highbury and made more than 50 first team appearances.

John Peart

Peart began his career with Woolwich Arsenal in December 1910 and left for Croydon Common in May 1914 on a free transfer. After four years in the Army, he returned to Arsenal in May 1919 for a two-year spell. He made more than 60 appearances in the red shirt of the club.

Ernie Tuckett

A centre-half, Tuckett signed for Arsenal in July 1932 but left for Margate to gain experience in August 1934. In March 1936, he returned to Arsenal but lost out to Herbie Roberts in the battle for the central defensive position. He left Arsenal for good in February 1937 in a deal that brought Laurie Scott to London from Bradford City.

Len Wills

He joined Arsenal in January 1946 but was called up for national service and when he was demobbed, he joined Crystal Palace. He returned to Highbury in 1949 but did not make his first-team debut until right-back Joe Wade was injured. Willis's first game was the north London derby against Spurs on 10 October 1953 and Arsenal won 4-1. He stayed at Arsenal for 13 years and made more than 200 appearances for the club before joining Romford in May 1962.

Bob Wilson

After capturing the number one jersey from Jim Furnell, Wilson was a safe pair of hands between the sticks for Arsenal, the club he had joined as an amateur in July 1963. In 1974, Wilson announced his retirement and joined the BBC as a television presenter. He continued to work at Arsenal as a goalkeeping coach little realising that in April 1978, a goalkeeping crisis meant that he would be re-registered as a player at Arsenal. Thankfully (for him), he was never called upon to play for the first team although he did turn out for the reserves.

Tom Winship

Outside-left Winship signed for Woolwich Arsenal in November 1910 and made his debut on Boxing Day against Manchester United. He lost the battle for his place and moved to Fulham in March 1913 but by August of that year he was back at Woolwich Arsenal. By the time the First World War erupted, he had played more than 5o games for the Gunners. He enrolled in the Army and made no contact with his former club. After demob, he signed for Darlington.

ARSENAL OLDIES

The oldest player to represent Arsenal is Jock Rutherford (1884-1963), who was 41 years and 159 days old when he appeared against Manchester City on 20 March 1926. In the Premier League, and also European competitions, the record for the oldest player is held by John Lukic (b. 1960). He was 39 years and 336 days old when he played for Arsenal against Derby County on Saturday 11 November 2000; and 25 days younger when he kept goal against Lazio in the Champions League group stage on Tuesday 17 October 2000.

THE ARSENAL – DECADE BY DECADE: 1960s

1960-61

First Division	P	W	D	L	F	A	W	D	L	F	A	Pts
11. Arsenal	42	12	3	6	44	35	3	8	10	33	50	41

FA Cup: Third round

1961-62

First Division	P	W	D	L	F	A	W	D	L	F	A	Pts
10. Arsenal	42	9	6	6	39	31	7	5	9	32	41	43

FA Cup: Fourth round

1962-63

First Division	P	W	D	L	F	A	W	D	L	F	A	Pts
7. Arsenal	42	11	4	6	44	33	7	6	8	42	44	46

FA Cup: Fifth round

1963-64

First Division	P	W	D	L	F	A	W	D	L	F	A	Pts
8. Arsenal	42	10	7	4	56	37	7	4	10	34	45	45

FA Cup: Fifth round
Europe: ICFC Second round

1964-65

First Division	P	W	D	L	F	A	W	D	L	F	A	Pts
13. Arsenal	42	11	5	5	42	31	6	2	13	27	44	41

FA Cup: Fourth round

1965-66

First Division	P	W	D	L	F	A	W	D	L	F	A	Pts
14. Arsenal	42	8	8	5	36	31	4	5	12	26	44	37

FA Cup: Third round

1966-67

First Division	P	W	D	L	F	A	W	D	L	F	A	Pts
7. Arsenal	42	11	6	4	32	20	5	8	8	26	27	46

FA Cup: Fifth round
League Cup: Third round

1967-68

First Division	P	W	D	L	F	A	W	D	L	F	A	Pts
9. Arsenal	42	12	6	3	37	23	5	4	12	23	33	44

FA Cup: Fifth round
League Cup: Runners-up

1968-69

First Division	P	W	D	L	F	A	W	D	L	F	A	Pts
4. Arsenal	42	12	6	3	31	12	10	6	5	25	15	56

FA Cup: Fifth round
League Cup: Runners-up

1969-70

First Division	P	W	D	L	F	A	W	D	L	F	A	Pts
12. Arsenal	42	7	10	4	29	23	5	8	8	22	26	42

FA Cup: Third round
League Cup: Third round
Europe: ICFC Winners

HALF A DOZEN CLEAN SHEETS

Only two Arsenal goalies have kept a clean sheet in first-team matches half a dozen times consecutively.

Jimmy Ashcroft: 1901-02

Ashcroft joined Woolwich Arsenal in June 1900 from Gravesend United. On 15 September 1900, he made his debut against Burton Swifts but Arsenal lost 1-0. He was ever-present in his first and second seasons and in the second season he kept 17 clean sheets in 34 matches including six in a row. In the 1903-04 season, he kept out the opposition 20 times. He also played 154 consecutive game for Arsenal, a run that ended in 1905-06.

Alex Manninger: 1997-98

The last of Manninger's clean sheets was against Manchester United at Old Trafford, where Arsenal won 1–0, a result that helped them beat United to the 1997–98 Premier League title, thereby winning the young Austrian the player of the month award, a first for an understudy goalkeeper in the Premier League.

UP FOR THE CUP – XIX

Arsenal 1 Sheffield Wednesday 1 aet

Less than a month after the League Cup Final clash, on Saturday 15 May 1993, the Gunners and the Owls met again at Wembley for the second cup final of the season. This time 79,347 fans watched the two teams play out a one-all draw (after extra time) in the FA Cup Final with Arsenal's solitary goal coming from Ian Wright who was playing with a broken toe. Luckily, he scored with his head. This was the first FA Cup final in which squad numbers had been used, having been trialled in the League Cup final. Players from both clubs used the same numbers for all three matches. The Premier League adopted the system for the following season. Arsenal: David Seaman, Lee Dixon, Nigel Winterburn, Paul Davis, Tony Adams (captain), Andy Linighan, John Jensen, Ray Parlour (Alan Smith), Paul Merson, Kevin Campbell, Ian Wright (David O'Leary).

Arsenal 2 Sheffield Wednesday 1 aet

On Monday 17 May 1993, before the replay could take place, a near full-strength Arsenal lined up against Manchester United for David O'Leary's testimonial game. Twenty-two thousand, one hundred and seventeen turned up to watch a 4-4 draw. On Thursday 20 May 1993, Arsenal and Sheffield Wednesday returned to Wembley for the FA Cup Final replay. Both FA Cup semi-finals were staged at Wembley, so the Gunners and the Owls each played there four times in six weeks – FA Cup semi-final, League Cup Final, FA Cup Final and replay. The replay attracted the smallest crowd (62,267) for an FA Cup Final at Wembley. The kick-off was put back half an hour because a crash on the M1 had delayed thousands of Wednesday fans. It was the first time a Wembley kick-off had not begun on time since the White Horse final in 1923. It was also chucking it down. In the early stages, Mark Bright went in roughly on Andy Linighan and broke the Arsenal man's nose. Ian Wright opened the scoring on 34 minutes putting Arsenal ahead as he had done in the first game but after 61 minutes Chris Waddle equalised for Wednesday and that was the way it stayed at 90 minutes. With just a minute of extra time remaining Andy Linighan won the game for Arsenal with a header. Arsenal: David Seaman, Lee Dixon, Nigel Winterburn, Paul Davis, Tony Adams (captain), Andy Linighan, John Jensen, Paul Davis, Kevin Campbell, Alan Smith, Paul Merson, Ian Wright (David O'Leary).

DISGUISE

In April 1927, Cardiff City became the first and so far only "foreign" side to win the FA Cup. Before that time, English clubs would secretly send scouts to spy on potential signings in Wales to stop the Welsh clubs from snapping them up. In the 1920s Arsenal were no different and would often send their men across the border but, if discovered, it was a fair bet that the Englishmen would be beaten up for their troubles. Sir Henry Norris arranged a series of less than elaborate disguises for his club's scouts. In 1922, Arsenal and Cardiff City were competing for the signature of Caerphilly Town's Bob John and thanks to the disguise Norris provided for manager Leslie Knighton, John signed for Arsenal in January 1922 for £750. He made his Arsenal first-team debut on Saturday 28 October 1922 in a 2-1 defeat at home to Newcastle United. Almost 80 years later, Arsène Wenger explained that he had used similar subterfuge in the signing of Cesc Fàbregas. "We even watched him in training. How did I do that? With a hat and moustache," explained the Frenchman.

PLAYED FOR ARSENAL ON THREE OCCASIONS

Tom Fitchie

Amateur Tom Fitchie joined Woolwich Arsenal in November 1901 from Queens Park Rangers but the next month joined Spurs. In February 1902, he was back at Woolwich Arsenal where he stayed for four years. He left for Fulham in February 1906 but was back for this third and final time at Woolwich Arsenal in September 1908. He played 56 league games and scored 27 goals.

Gordon Hoare

In May 1907, he joined Woolwich Arsenal and remained for two and a half years before leaving for Glossop. In December 1910, he returned to Woolwich Arsenal before returning to Glossop again in February 1912. It was while at Glossop on 4 July 1912 that he won an Olympic Gold Medal as part of England's winning side at the Stockholm Olympics. In March 1914 he returned to the club that had a new name – no longer Woolwich Arsenal – and a new home – Highbury. In August 1914, he was off again and this time there was no return.

Hugh McDonald

Born in Kilwinning, Ayrshire, he joined Woolwich Arsenal in January 1906 where he was deputy to Jimmy Ashcroft, the club's first England international. Ashcroft's form limited McDonald to just two appearances – his debut coming on 17 February 1906 against Blackburn Rovers. At the end of that season, he left to join Brighton & Hove Albion where he spent two years. In May 1908, McDonald returned to Woolwich Arsenal after the club sold Ashcroft. McDonald was ever-present in 1908-09 and missed just two games the following season. He left Arsenal in July 1910 for Oldham Athletic. In December 1912, he was back between the sticks for Woolwich Arsenal replacing Harold Crawford in 18 of the last 21 games for the 1912-13 season. It was not a happy time as Arsenal were relegated for the only time in their history. In November 1913, McDonald lost his place to Joe Lievesley and so left to join Fulham

Jim Quayle

Quayle had three spells at Woolwich Arsenal – two as an amateur and one as a professional. He joined in August 1907, left two months later to sign for Fleetwood, returned to Arsenal in June 1908 and left again for Fleetwood four months later. In October 1910 he signed professional terms with Woolwich Arsenal but in his first match against Sheffield Wednesday on 12 November 1910 he was so badly injured that he was forced to retire.

Jock Rutherford

He joined Woolwich Arsenal a month after the move to north London and stayed six years although war service interrupted the continuity. In 1919, he signed for Chelsea and then moved to Stoke City as player-manager. In September 1923, he returned to Arsenal and stayed for 20 months before announcing his retirement in May 1925. He returned to Arsenal in January 1926 for a further six-month's service. He played more than 300 times for Arsenal.

LE PROF SPEAKS – III

"Despite global warming, England is still not warm enough for him."
On José Antonio Reyes's leaving, 2007

BATTLE OF BRITAIN IN EUROPE

Arsenal have been drawn against teams from the British Isles on just three occasions in Europe – the first time was against Irish side Glentoran is the only ocassion they've been successful, and they've never won against English opponents. These are the results.

Season	Competition	Opponents	Home	Away
1969-70	ICFC	Glentoran	3-0	0-1
2003-04	ECL	Chelsea	1-2	1-1
2007-08	ECL	Liverpool	1-1	2-4

THE ARSENAL – DECADE BY DECADE: 1970s

1970-71

First Division	P	W	D	L	F	A	W	D	L	F	A	Pts
1. Arsenal	42	18	3	0	41	6	11	4	6	30	23	65

FA Cup: Winners
League Cup: Fourth round
Europe: ICFC Fourth round

1971-72

First Division	P	W	D	L	F	A	W	D	L	F	A	Pts
5. Arsenal	42	15	2	4	36	13	7	6	8	22	27	52

FA Cup: Runners-up
League Cup: Fourth round
Europe: ECC Third round

1972-73

First Division	P	W	D	L	F	A	W	D	L	F	A	Pts
2. Arsenal	42	14	5	2	31	14	9	6	6	26	29	57

FA Cup: Semi-finalist
League Cup: Fifth round

1973-74

First Division	P	W	D	L	F	A	W	D	L	F	A	Pts
10. Arsenal	42	9	7	5	23	16	5	7	9	26	35	42

FA Cup: Fourth round
League Cup: Second round

1974-75

First Division	P	W	D	L	F	A	W	D	L	F	A	Pts
16. Arsenal	42	10	6	5	31	16	3	5	13	16	33	37

FA Cup: Sixth round
League Cup: Second round

1975-76

First Division	P	W	D	L	F	A	W	D	L	F	A	Pts
13. Arsenal	42	11	4	6	33	19	2	6	13	14	34	36

FA Cup: Third round
League Cup: Second round

1976-77

First Division	P	W	D	L	F	A	W	D	L	F	A	Pts
8. Arsenal	42	11	6	4	37	20	5	5	11	27	39	43

FA Cup: Fifth round
League Cup: Fifth round

1977-78

First Division	P	W	D	L	F	A	W	D	L	F	A	Pts
5. Arsenal	42	14	5	2	38	12	7	5	9	22	25	52

FA Cup: Runners-up
League Cup: Semi-final

1978-79

First Division	P	W	D	L	F	A	W	D	L	F	A	Pts
7. Arsenal	42	11	8	2	37	18	6	6	9	24	30	48

FA Cup: Winners
League Cup: Second round
Europe: UC Third round

1979-80

First Division	P	W	D	L	F	A	W	D	L	F	A	Pts
4. Arsenal	42	8	10	3	24	12	10	6	5	28	24	52

FA Cup: Runners-up
League Cup: Fifth round
Europe: ECWC Runners-up

UP FOR THE CUP – XX

Arsenal 1 Parma 0

On Wednesday 4 May 1994, Arsenal met Parma (managed by Sven-Göran Eriksson) in the European Cup Winners' Cup Winners Final in Copenhagen's Parken Stadium. It was a chance for the team to make up for their defeat in the same competition 14 years earlier. Ian Wright was unable to play because a yellow card in the semi-final against Paris St Germain meant that he was suspended while John Jensen was out with an injury. David Hillier and Martin Keown were also missing and Seaman played with a pain-killing injection in his ribs. Parma, the holders of the trophy, were favourites to retain the trophy. Only 33,765 fans watched Alan Smith score Arsenal's winner on 21 minutes. Once they had the goal, Arsenal's defence put up the shutters as they so often did and Parma in all yellow with blue trim found that they could not break them down. Arsenal: David Seaman, Lee Dixon, Nigel Winterburn, Paul Davis, Steve Bould, Tony Adams (captain), Ian Selley, Steve Morrow, Paul Merson (Eddie McGoldrick), Kevin Campbell, Alan Smith.

ARSENAL'S YOUNGEST

Francesc Fàbregas (b. 1987) is Arsenal's youngest player, making his debut at 16 years and 177 days in a 1-1 draw against Rotherham United in the League Cup Third Round on 28 October 2003. (Arsenal won 9-8 on penalties.) Fàbregas is also Arsenal's youngest ever player in the Premier League – he was 17 years 103 days when he appeared against Everton (at Goodison Park) on Sunday 15 August 2004; and the youngest scorer against Blackburn Rovers on Wednesday 25 August 2004 when he was 17 years and 113 days. He is also Arsenal's youngest player in Europe. He was 17 years and 169 days old when he played in the away leg 2-2 draw against Panathinaikos on Wednesday 20 October 2004. The youngest player in the old First Division was Gerry Ward (1936-1994) on 22 August 1953 at Highbury against Huddersfield Town in a 0-0 draw. Stewart Robson (b. 1964) holds the record for the youngest player in the FA Cup when he played against Spurs on 2 January 1982. He was 17 years and 55 days old. Arsenal lost 1-0.

AROUND THE WORLD

Several international clubs have been inspired by the Gunners.

Arsenal de Sarandí (Argentina)

Based in Avellaneda, a suburb of Buenos Aires, Arsenal were founded on 11 January 1957 by the brothers Héctor and Julio Humberto Grondona. The London club directly influenced them. The club, nicknamed El Viaducto (after their ground) or El Arse, were promoted to the Argentine Premier League in 2002.

Berekum Arsenal (Ghana)

Founded in 1978, their kit is the same as the Gunners' as is their club motto. They play in the Ghana Telecom Premier League.

Arsenal (Lesotho)

This Arsenal, based in Maseru, play in the Lesotho Premier League. They have a cannon on their badge along with the legend Gunners L.C.

FK Arsenal (Montenegro)

Founded in 1919, Fudbalski Klub Arsenal play at Tivat in the Montenegrin second division.

FK Arsenal (Serbia)

Playing in Kragujevac, Arsenal play in the same red shirts, white sleeves and shorts as the Emirates side.

Arsenal Kiev (Ukraine)

Founded in 1934, originally called CSKA Kiev, they play in the Ukrainian Premier League. The club was in financial difficulties until the oligarch Vadim Rabynovich bought it.

In addition to the clubs above there are four other clubs across the globe founded under the influence of Arsenal. Arsenal Kharkiv, who play in League B in Ukraine; Arsenal (Honduras), founded in 1999, they play in Roatan in the Liga de Ascenso; Arsenal (Russia), who play at Arsenal Stadium, which was built in 1959 in Tula; and Arsenal Wanderers, a second division team in Belle Vue, Maurtius.

ARSENAL FIRSTS

Arsenal's first recognised fixture was a friendly against Eastern Wanderers on Saturday 11 December 1886. While their first FA Cup match was against Lyndhurst on Saturday 5 October 1889 and they won 11-0.

Arsenal were the first southern team to turn professional and also the first football team to issue shares (in 1893).

The first league match as Woolwich Arsenal was played at the Manor Ground Plumstead on Saturday 2 September 1893, against Newcastle United. The match ended 2-2 with the goals scored by Walter Shaw and Arthur Elliott in front of a crowd of 10,000. Shaw (1870-1933) scored Arsenal's first league goal.

Joe Heath scored the club's first hat-trick in league football against Walsall Town Swifts on 11 September 1893 when Woolwich Arsenal won 4-0.

In 1894-95 Jack Caldwell became the first player to ever present in a league season for the club.

The first away league match was against Notts County on Saturday 9 September 1893. Woolwich Arsenal lost 3-2 with the goals scored by Arthur Elliott and Walter Shaw. The first league win was on Monday 11 September 1893 when they beat Walsall Town Swifts 4-0 and John Heath scored a hat-trick.

Arsenal's first FA Cup match (played at Manor Ground, Plumstead) was against Ashford United on Saturday 14 October 1893 and the club won 12-0 with goals from Arthur Elliott 3, Jim Henderson 3, Charlie Booth 2, Joe Heath 2, Gavin Crawford and Joe Powell.

On 13 April 1895 Arsenal goalie Harry Storer became the first player to gain representative honours when he played for the Football League against the Scottish League.

Caesar Jenkyns was Arsenal's first international player. He played for Wales in their 4-0 defeat by Scotland on 21 March 1896.

The 1903-04 season was the first Arsenal were unbeaten at home. The following season, Charlie Satterthwaite scored Arsenal's first goal in the First Division – against Wolves on 24 September 1904.

Jimmy Ashcroft was Arsenal's first England international when he played in the Home Championships against Ireland in 1906.

Arsenal were the first team to be run by a football "tsar" (Sir Henry Norris; 1865-1934) from 1910.

Woolwich Arsenal's first game at Highbury was a 2-1 victory over Leicester Fosse in a Second Division fixture on Saturday 6 September 1913. George Jobey and Danny Devine (penalty) scored the goals.

The first competitive match as Arsenal was a 1-1 draw at home to Bristol City on Saturday 4 April 1914. Tom Winship scored.

The first match to be broadcast live on the wireless was Arsenal v Sheffield United on Saturday 22 January 1927. And the first live goal on the wireless by Arsenal was scored by Charles Buchan.

In October 1928, David Jack was the first player to be sold for a five-figure sum when he joined Arsenal from Bolton Wanderers.

Arsenal and Sheffield Wednesday became the first teams to wear numbers on their backs in a league match on Saturday 25 August 1928. The system that day (until 1939) used numbers 1-22.

The 1930 FA Cup Final between Arsenal and Huddersfield was the first time in a major match in which the two captains came out side by side.

Arsenal's first match in the Charity Shield was against Sheffield Wednesday on Thursday 8 October 1931 (at Stamford Bridge). Arsenal won 2-1 with goals from Joe Hulme and David Jack.

In the 1932 FA Cup Final, Arsenal became were the first team to score first at Wembley and still lose. In November of the same year the first match under floodlights was played at Highbury.

The first match in which Arsenal wore red shirts with white sleeves was against Liverpool at Highbury on 4 March 1933. The Gunners lost 1-0.

In 1934-35, Arsenal became the first club to have gate receipts of more than £100,000 in a season (profits of £35,000).

The first match to be broadcast live on television was Arsenal v Arsenal Reserves on Thursday 16 September 1937.

In 1950, Arsenal became the first club to win the FA Cup without leaving London during the run.

In 1958, Jack Kelsey and Dave Bowen became the first Arsenal players to appear in the World Cup finals.

Arsenal's first away match in European competition was against Staevnet (Denmark) on Wednesday 25 September 1963 in the Inter-Cities Fairs Cup. Arsenal won 7-1 with Geoff Strong 3, Joe Baker 3, and Johnny MacLeod hitting the net. Arsenal's first home match in European competition was against Staevnet (Denmark) on Tuesday 22 October 1963 in the Inter-Cities Fairs Cup. Arsenal lost 3-2 with goals from Alan Skirton and John Barnwell.

Liverpool 3 Arsenal 2 at Anfield was the first (and only) game featured on *Match of the Day* on its first episode on Saturday 22 August 1964.

Alan Skirton became Arsenal's first substitute on 28 September 1965 when he replaced Jon Sammels in a match against Northampton Town.

Arsenal's first League Cup match was on Tuesday 13 September 1966 at home to Gillingham. Tommy Baldwin scored Arsenal's goal in a 1-1 draw.

Arsenal's first six-figure transfer fee was £100,000 paid out on Friday 2 January 1970 to buy Peter Marinello from Hibernian.

On Saturday 11 March 1972, Brendon Batson became the first black player to represent Arsenal when he came on as a substitute against Newcastle United at St James' Park. Arsenal lost 2-0.

In 1979-80, Arsenal became the first English side to play 70 competitive games in a season. That season Pat Rice became the first player to appear in five FA Cup Finals for the same club, and, on 23 April 1980, Arsenal became the first British club to beat Juventus in Turin.

Arsenal's first match in the Premier League was at home to Norwich City on Saturday 15 August 1992. The Gunners lost 4-2 with goals scored by Steve Bould and Kevin Campbell. That season Arsenal became the first team to win both major domestic cups in the same season and in doing so George Graham became the first man to win the championship and two domestic cups as a player and a manager.

Arsenal's first match in the Champions League was away to RC Lens on Wednesday 16 September 1998: a 1-1 draw, Marc Overmars scored.

In October 1998, Remi Garde was the first foreign captain of Arsenal. While Tony Adams is the first Arsenal player to win league championship medals in three different decades and the first Arsenal player to captain the side to two doubles.

Arsenal won (1-0), the first "indoor" FA Cup Final. Due to heavy rain, the roof on the Millennium Stadium was closed for the 2003 Final against Southampton. Arsenal also won the first final decided on penalties when they beat Manchester United 5-4 in the 2005 match.

On Tuesday 21 February 2006, Arsenal were the first English team to beat Real Madrid at the Santiago Bernabeu on the way to becoming the first team from London to reach the European Champions League Final at the end of that season.

The first goal scored at Emirates Stadium was from Klaas Jan Huntelaar of Ajax in Dennis Bergkamp's testimonial match in July 2006. The first Premier League goal scored for Arsenal was by Gilberto Silva on 19 August 2006 against Aston Villa. The first goal scored by an Englishman was by Justin Hoyte on Tuesday 2 January 2007 against Charlton Athletic.

On Tuesday 4 March 2008, Arsenal became the first English team to beat AC Milan at the San Siro.

SIGHT UNSEEN

It is usual for a manager – or a scout – to watch a player several times before signing him. Arsène Wenger isn't known for rash decisions, which made the signing of Freddie Ljungberg even more unusual. He signed the midfielder for £3million after watching him on television playing for Sweden against England. Ljungberg lived up to Wenger's expectations, playing more than 300 games for the club before joining West Ham in 2007.

EARLY FILM STARS

In 1931, the BBC approached Herbert Chapman to ask if his team would participate in a short film to be shown in cinemas in London. Chapman agreed to the suggestion and the players (all except Alex James who declared, "I'm not a performing seal") lined up to be introduced by Tom Whittaker before they broke into a chorus of 'Good Company'.

ARSENAL IN NUMBERS

3	League and Cup doubles
3	Percentage of the Emirates Stadium pitch that is plastic grass.
5	European finals
10	FA Cup wins
10	initial subscription cost in guineas for the Enclosure Club
12	International matches played at Highbury
13	League titles
16	Number of players used in the first double season
25	Number of players used in the third double season
26	Number of players used in the second double season
44	Pints of paint used for white lines for each game at the Emirates
49	Most consecutive League matches without defeat
109×73	Highbury pitch size in yards
113x74	Emirates Stadium pitch size in yards
£2,000	Herbert Chapman's initial salary as Arsenal manager
4,554	Lowest First Division Highbury attendance (5 May 1966)
38,419	Highbury capacity after Taylor Report into hooliganism
59,900	Average attendance at Emirates in its first season
60,355	Emirates Stadium capacity

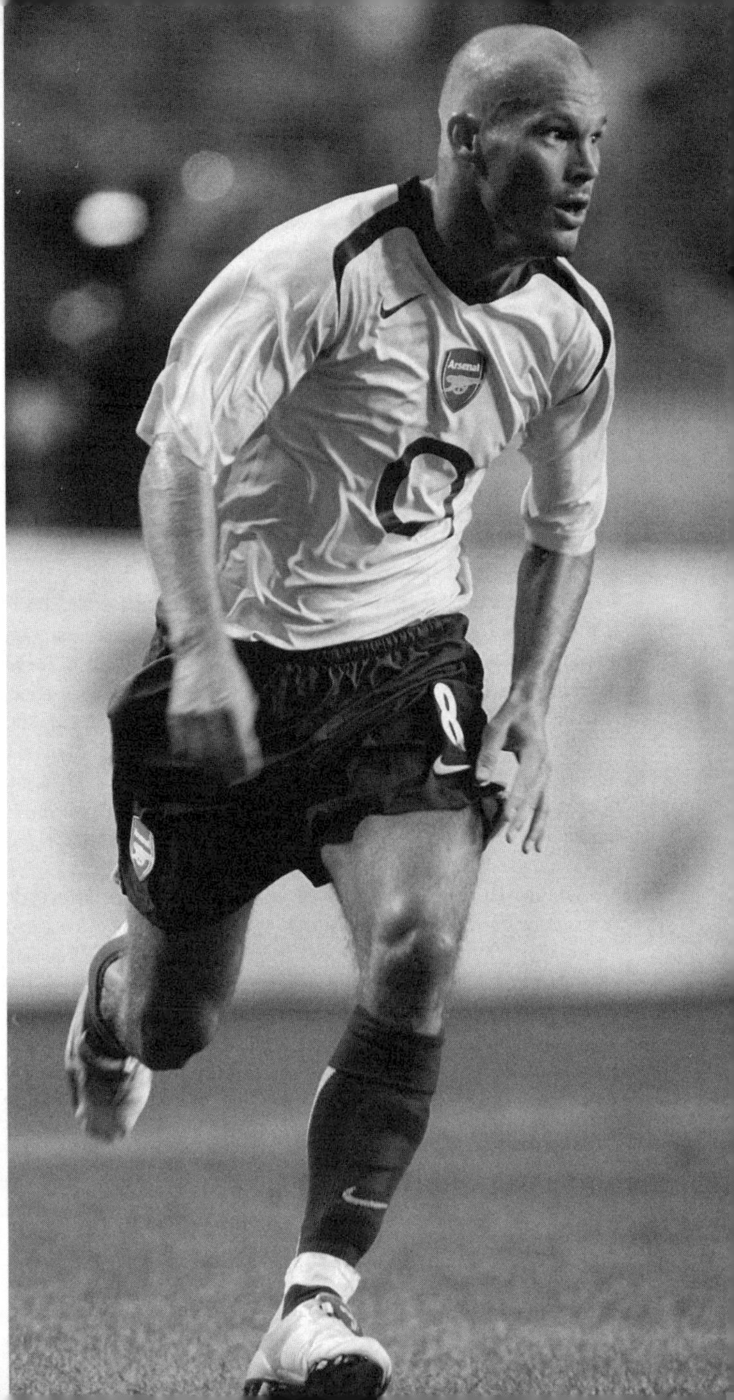

BOUGHT UNSEEN: FREDDIE LJUNGBERG

OUTFIELD PLAYERS BETWEEN THE STICKS

Joe Baker

On 31 August 1963, goalie Jack McClelland was injured after 22 minutes of a match against Leicester City with the Gunners trailing 2-0. Centre-forward Baker volunteered to go in goal but despite his best efforts the boys from Filbert Street put another five past him and the Gunners went down 7-2.

Wally Barnes

Full-back Barnes joined Arsenal in September 1943 and in his 12 years at the club played in every position except centre-forward. On 10 April 1944, he even played in goal against Brighton & Hove Albion in a Football League South game. Arsenal won 3-1.

James Boyle

Boyle joined Arsenal from Clyde in November 1893 and over the course of the next four years, he played more than 60 games for Arsenal scoring seven league goals. A versatile player, he appeared in eight different positions during his Arsenal career and even kept goal in four league games in December 1895 but let in eight goals in two wins and two defeats.

Leslie Compton

During the Second World War, he often played in goal for Arsenal.

Eddie Hapgood

On Saturday 16 March 1935, Arsenal played Everton at Goodison Park. Attempting to foil an Everton attack, goalie Frank Moss dislocated his shoulder. Trainer Tom Whittaker treated him and Eddie Hapgood went in goal while Moss moved to outside-left on his return to the field of play. By that time Arsenal were leading 1-0. Later in the match, Moss found himself in the centre of the pitch, trapped a cross and hit it into the back of the Everton net. Moments later, he went to hospital.

John Radford

For the second year in succession Arsenal were drawn against Stoke City in the FA Cup Semi Final and for the second year in succession, the match had to be decided by a replay. In the first match on Saturday 15 April

1972 at Villa Park Arsenal goalie Bob Wilson was injured and unable to continue despite receiving "encouragement" from teammate Peter Storey (what ITV commentator Brian Moore used to call "giving him stick"). John Radford went in goal while substitute Ray Kennedy moved into Radford's position. Thanks to a goal from George Armstrong, Arsenal managed to hang on for a replay at Goodison Park on Wednesday 19 April, which they won 2-1 with goals from Charlie George (penalty) and John Radford. Geoff Barnett took over in goal against a Stoke side that included Gordon Banks and ex-Gunner George Eastham.

UP FOR THE CUP – XXI

Arsenal 0 AC Milan 0

On 1 February 1995, Arsenal met AC Milan at Highbury before a crowd of 38,044 in the first leg of the 1994 European Super Cup – the contest between the winners of the European Cup and the European Cup Winners' Cup. AC Milan, managed by future England boss Fabio Capello, had won the European Cup convincingly beating Barcelona 4-0 on 18 May 1994 at the Athens Olympic Stadium in Greece. The previous year they had lost the Super Cup to Parma who had, of course, beaten Arsenal. (Interestingly, Arsenal lost consecutive European finals to teams managed by future England managers.) The Italian side came to Highbury determined to avenge their defeat and to not let the Gunners play. They succeeded returning to Milan having achieved a 0-0 draw. Arsenal: David Seaman, Lee Dixon, Nigel Winterburn, Stefan Schwarz, Steve Bould, Tony Adams (captain), John Jensen (David Hillier), Ian Wright, John Hartson, Ian Selley, Kevin Campbell (Paul Merson).

AC Milan 2 Arsenal 0

A week later, Arsenal were at the San Siro for the second leg. With no away goals conceded George Graham's men were confident that they could snatch one in Milan. Zvonimir Boban had other ideas and on 41 minutes, he put AC Milan into the lead. With 67 minutes on the clock Daniele Massaro who had scored twice against Barcelona popped up to score Milan's second and clinch them their third Super Cup in six years. Arsenal: David Seaman, Lee Dixon (Martin Keown), Nigel Winterburn, Stefan Schwarz, Steve Bould, Tony Adams (captain), Kevin Campbell (Ray Parlour), Ian Wright, John Hartson, Paul Merson, Ian Selley.

THE ARSENAL – DECADE BY DECADE: 1980s

1980-81

First Division	P	W	D	L	F	A	W	D	L	F	A	Pts
3. Arsenal	42	13	8	0	36	17	6	7	8	25	28	53

FA Cup: Third round
League Cup: Fourth round

1981-82

First Division	P	W	D	L	F	A	W	D	L	F	A	Pts
5. Arsenal	42	13	5	3	27	15	7	6	8	21	22	71

FA Cup: Third round
League Cup: Fourth round
Europe: UC Second round

1982-83

First Division	P	W	D	L	F	A	W	D	L	F	A	Pts
10. Arsenal	42	11	6	4	36	19	5	4	12	22	37	58

FA Cup: Semi-final
League Cup: Semi-final
Europe: UC First round

1983-84

First Division	P	W	D	L	F	A	W	D	L	F	A	Pts
6. Arsenal	42	10	5	6	41	29	8	4	9	33	31	63

FA Cup: Third round
League Cup: Fourth round

1984-85

First Division	P	W	D	L	F	A	W	D	L	F	A	Pts
7. Arsenal	42	14	5	2	37	14	5	4	12	24	35	66

FA Cup: Fourth round
League Cup: Third round

1985-86

First Division	P	W	D	L	F	A	W	D	L	F	A	Pts
7. Arsenal	42	13	5	3	29	15	7	4	10	20	32	69

FA Cup: Fifth round
League Cup: Quarter-final

1986-87

First Division	P	W	D	L	F	A	W	D	L	F	A	Pts
4. Arsenal	42	12	5	4	31	12	8	5	8	27	23	70

FA Cup: Sixth round
League Cup: Winners

1987-88

First Division	P	W	D	L	F	A	W	D	L	F	A	Pts
6. Arsenal	40	11	4	5	35	16	7	8	5	23	23	66

FA Cup: Sixth round
League Cup: Runners-up

1988-89

First Division	P	W	D	L	F	A	W	D	L	F	A	Pts
1. Arsenal	38	10	6	3	35	19	12	4	3	38	17	76

FA Cup: Third round
League Cup: Third round

1989-90

First Division	P	W	D	L	F	A	W	D	L	F	A	Pts
4. Arsenal	38	14	3	2	38	11	4	5	10	16	27	62

FA Cup: Fourth round
League Cup: Fourth round

UP FOR THE CUP – XXII

Arsenal 1 Real Zaragoza 2

On 10 May 1995, Arsenal played Real Zaragoza at the Parc des Princes in Paris defending their European Cup Winners' Cup before 42,424 spectators. With George Graham's sacking, Stewart Houston took charge of the team. John Hartson scored for Arsenal, equalising after Juan Esnáider had put the Spaniards ahead. At 90 minutes, the referee blew for full time and an extra 30 minutes loomed. With penalties looming, on the 120th minute ex-Spurs player Nayim spotted that Seaman was off his line and lobbed him from 40 yards winning the game for Real Zaragoza. Arsenal: David Seaman, Lee Dixon, Nigel Winterburn (Steve Morrow), Andy Linighan, Tony Adams (captain), Martin Keown (David Hillier), Stefan Schwarz, Ray Parlour, Paul Merson, John Hartson, Ian Wright.

UP FOR THE CUP – XXIII

Arsenal 2 Newcastle United 0

On Saturday 16 May 1998, Arsenal returned to Wembley for the FA Cup Final, against Newcastle United. Dennis Bergkamp was missing through a hamstring injury but most neutrals still expected Arsenal to win and complete their second double, in Arsène Wenger's first full season in charge. And so it proved: Marc Overmars and Nicolas Anelka scored Arsenal's goals in the 23rd and 69th minutes respectively before 79,183 fans. Arsenal: David Seaman, Lee Dixon, Nigel Winterburn, Patrick Vieira, Martin Keown, Tony Adams (captain), Emmanuel Petit, Ray Parlour, Marc Overmars, Christopher Wreh (David Platt), Nicolas Anelka.

ARSENAL LASTS

The last game Arsenal played in the Second Division was against Nottingham Forest on Saturday 24 April 1915. The Gunners won 7-0.

The last amateur to play football for England was Bernard Joy of Arsenal, on Saturday 9 May 1936 against Belgium.

The last season during which Arsenal shirts did not bear a sponsor's name was 1981-1982, while the last season in which you could stand at Arsenal Stadium was 1992-1993.

The last signing made by George Graham was Dutchman Glenn Helder in February 1995 – but Graham was fired before he could pick him.

The last Arsenal goalkeeper to score was Graham Stack on 26 October 2003. He hit the back of the net with a penalty in the 9-8 shootout against Rotherham United in the League Cup.

Kolo Touré scored the last goal under lights at Highbury, against Villareal on 19 April 2006 in the first leg of the Champions League semi-final. The last match played at Highbury was on Sunday 7 May 2006 against Wigan Athletic and Arsenal won 4-2, which featured the last hat-trick to be scored on the ground, by Thierry Henry.

PLAYERS WHO STOOD MORE THAN 6FT 2IN

Tony Adams...6ft 3in
Emmanuel Adebayor 6ft 3in
Ted Batcup..6ft 3in
Johan Djourou-Gbadjere 6ft 3in
Jens Lehmann...................................6ft 3in
Alan Miller 6ft 3in
Bill Patterson 6ft 3in
Gilberto Silva...................................6ft 3in
George Wood 6ft 3in
Willie Young.....................................6ft 3in
Steve Bould......................................6ft 4in
Pascal Cygan....................................6ft 4in
Jim Fotheringham............................6ft 4in
John Lukic 6ft 4in
Rami Shaaban...................................6ft 4in
Igor Stepanovs 6ft 4in
Patrick Vieira 6ft 4in
Mart Poom 6ft 4½in
Niall Quinn......................................6ft 5in
Stuart Taylor 6ft 5in

UP FOR THE CUP – XXIV

Arsenal 0 Galatasary 0 (1-4 on penalties)

On Wednesday 17 May 2000, Arsenal played Galatasaray in the Uefa Cup Final at the Parken Stadium, Copenhagen before a crowd of 38,919 supporters. It was an extremely tight affair, and the score at full-time was 0-0. After a further 30 minutes' extra-time, in which neither side were able to break the deadlock, the match was decided by a penalty shoot-out. It was a disaster for the Gunners, as Arsenal could not seem to get their goal-scoring act together and Galatasaray won 4-1. It was the first European trophy won by a Turkish club. Arsenal: David Seaman, Lee Dixon, Silvinho, Patrick Vieira, Martin Keown, Tony Adams (captain), Emmanuel Petit, Ray Parlour, Marc Overmars (Davor Šuker), Dennis Bergkamp (Nwankwo Kanu), Thierry Henry.

NEILL v GRAHAM: A COMPARATIVE RECORD

Terry Neill and George Graham are the only two men to have both played for and managed Arsenal and Spurs. Both men were sacked by Arsenal although only Graham was sacked by Spurs. A problem faced by Terry Neill was that some of the players he had to manage had been his team mates and whilst they liked him as a man, they were less keen on him as their boss. A similar problem arose for George Graham – some of the older players had been his golf buddies. He told them that it was all right to call him "George" the first time but they should not repeat the mistake and the next time they should call him "Boss". Neill joined Arsenal in December 1959 from Bangor and scored on his debut on 23 December 1960 in a 1-1 draw against Sheffield Wednesday. At the age of 19, he became Arsenal's youngest captain. He played 275 times for the Gunners before joining Hull City as player-manager in 1970 for a £40,000 fee. In 1974, he succeeded Bill Nicholson as manager of Spurs. On 9 July 1976 he became Arsenal's youngest ever manager replacing Bertie Mee after being head-hunted by the board. George Graham joined Arsenal as a player in October 1966 from Chelsea in a move that saw Tommy Baldwin move to Stamford Bridge. In six years at Arsenal Stadium, he won a League championship medal, an FA Cup winner's medal, a runner's up medal, a Fairs Cup winner's medal, and two League Cup runner's up medals. In the 1971 FA Cup Final he won the man of the match award. He left Arsenal in December 1972 for Manchester United for £120,000 following the arrival of Alan Ball. He became manager of Arsenal on 14 May 1986, after a successful spell in the chair at Millwall. After his year-long ban, imposed by the FA after the bung scandal, ended Graham became manager of Leeds United on Tuesday 10 September 1996. After two years at Elland Road, he left on Wednesday 30 September 1998 (being replaced by his assistant David O'Leary) and he was appointed Spurs chief. On Friday 16 March 2001, Lillywhites chairman Daniel Levy sacked him. Terry Neill led Arsenal to three successive FA Cup Finals from 1978 to 1980 but the team only won one and to the European Cup Winners' Cup Final in 1980 when they lost after Graham Rix missed a penalty against Valencia. He did not win any trophies at White Hart Lane. As manager of Arsenal, George Graham won two First Division Championships, one FA Cup, one League Cup and one European trophy (European Cup Winners Cup).

At Spurs he led Arsenal's greatest enemy to a League Cup triumph, their first trophy in nine years. Who knows what might have happened if he hadn't become embroiled in "financial irregularities"? We may never have heard of a Frenchman called Arsène Wenger and fans could be watching a mostly British Arsenal team claiming 1-0 wins from the comfort of the Chapman-Graham stand.

Terry Neill's managerial record

	P	W	D	L	F	A	P	W	D	L	F	A
Spurs v Arsenal	2	1	1	0	2	0	2	1	0	1	2	1

	P	W	D	L	F	A	P	W	D	L	F	A
Arsenal v Spurs	6	5	0	1	8	3	6	2	2	2	11	12

George Graham's managerial record

	P	W	D	L	F	A	P	W	D	L	F	A
Arsenal v Spurs	8	4	3	1	9	5	9	4	2	3	10	9

	P	W	D	L	F	A	P	W	D	L	F	A
Spurs v Arsenal	3	1	1	1	4	5	2	0	1	1	1	2

UP FOR THE CUP – XXV

Arsenal 1 Liverpool 2

With Wembley being demolished, the FA Cup Final moved to the magnificent Millennium Stadium in Cardiff on Saturday 12 May 2001 – it proved a happy hunting ground for the Gunners, but not in the first final to be played outside of England. Oddly, in a reverse of the 1971 Final, Liverpool wore gold and blue and Arsenal played in their usual red (and white). With 72 minutes on the clock, Freddie Ljungberg opened the scoring but two goals by Michael Owen broke Arsenal's heart and the trophy went to Liverpool. The attendance was 72,400. Arsenal: David Seaman, Lee Dixon (Dennis Bergkamp), Martin Keown, Tony Adams (captain), Ashley Cole, Patrick Vieira, Gilles Grimandi, Freddie Ljungberg (Nwankwo Kanu), Sylvain Wiltord (Ray Parlour), Thierry Henry, Robert Pirès

THE ARSENAL – DECADE BY DECADE: 1990s

1990-91

First Division	P	W	D	L	F	A	W	D	L	F	A	Pts
1. Arsenal	38	15	4	0	51	10	9	9	1	23	8	83*

FA Cup: Semi-final
League Cup: Fourth round

2pts deducted

1991-92

First Division	P	W	D	L	F	A	W	D	L	F	A	Pts
4. Arsenal	42	12	7	2	51	23	7	8	6	30	24	72

FA Cup: Third round
League Cup: Third round

Europe: UC Second round

1992-93

Premier League	P	W	D	L	F	A	W	D	L	F	A	Pts
10. Arsenal	42	8	6	7	25	20	7	5	9	15	18	56

FA Cup: Winners
League Cup: Winners

1993-94

Premier League	P	W	D	L	F	A	W	D	L	F	A	Pts
4. Arsenal	42	10	8	3	25	15	8	9	4	28	13	71

FA Cup: Fourth round
League Cup: Fourth round

Europe: ECWC Winners

1994-95

Premier League	P	W	D	L	F	A	W	D	L	F	A	Pts
12. Arsenal	42	6	9	6	27	21	7	3	11	25	28	51

FA Cup: Third round
League Cup: Quarter-final

Europe: ECWC Runners-up

1995-96

Premier League	P	W	D	L	F	A	W	D	L	F	A	Pts
4. Arsenal	38	10	7	2	30	16	7	5	7	19	16	63

FA Cup: Third round
League Cup: Semi-final

1996-97

Premier League	P	W	D	L	F	A	W	D	L	F	A	Pts
3. Arsenal	38	10	5	4	36	18	9	6	4	26	14	68

FA Cup: Fourth round
League Cup: Fourth round Europe: UC First round

1997-98

Premier League	P	W	D	L	F	A	W	D	L	F	A	Pts
1. Arsenal	38	15	2	2	43	10	8	7	4	25	23	78

FA Cup: Winners
League Cup: Semi-final Europe: UC First round

1998-99

Premier League	P	W	D	L	F	A	W	D	L	F	A	Pts
2. Arsenal	38	14	5	0	34	5	8	7	4	25	12	78

FA Cup: Semi-final
League Cup: Fourth round Europe: UCL First phase

1999-2000

Premier League	P	W	D	L	F	A	W	D	L	F	A	Pts
2. Arsenal	38	14	3	2	42	17	8	4	7	31	26	73

FA Cup: Fourth round
League Cup: Fourth round Europe: UCL First phase/UC Runners-up

UP FOR THE CUP – XXV

Arsenal 2 Chelsea 0

On Saturday 4 May 2002, Arsenal returned to the Millennium Stadium in Cardiff for their second consecutive FA Cup Final determined to avenge the defeat a year earlier by Liverpool. Ray Parlour scored first on 70 minutes and 10 minutes later Freddie Ljungberg made it 2-0 to the Gunners. Ljungberg, having also scored in the 2001 final, became the first man to score goals in successive FA Cup finals since Bobby Smith of Tottenham Hotspur, who scored in 1961 and 1962. The attendance was 73,963. The victory gave Arsenal their third double.Arsenal: David Seaman, Lauren, Sol Campbell, Tony Adams (captain), Ashley Cole, Patrick Vieira, Ray Parlour, Freddie Ljungberg, Sylvain Wiltord (Martin Keown), Dennis Bergkamp (Edu), Thierry Henry (Nwankwo Kanu).

UP FOR THE CUP – XXVI

Arsenal 1 Southampton 0

In a repeat of 1978-80, Arsenal returned to three consecutive FA Cup Finals. On Saturday 17 May 2003, they faced Southampton. There were 73,726 spectators at the match and, due to poor weather, the game was effectively played indoors. David Seaman, in his last appearance for the club, donned the captain's armband. Sol Campbell did not play after being sent off against Manchester United and Patrick Vieira was missing through a knee injury also obtained in the same match against United. Keown and Luzhny only played after being passed fit on the morning of the game. Arsenal wore their usual red and white strip but as with the game against Liverpool two years earlier, their opponents wore what had been Arsenal's normal away strip of yellow and blue. The game has quickly been forgotten but Robert Pirès scored the winning goal in the 38th minute. Arsenal: David Seaman (captain), Lauren, Martin Keown, Oleg Luzhny, Ashley Cole, Gilberto, Ray Parlour, Freddie Ljungberg, Robert Pirès, Dennis Bergkamp (Sylvain Wiltord), Thierry Henry.

ARSENAL ONLYS

George Morrell is the only Arsenal boss to have seen his team relegated.

Arsenal and Leicester City are the only teams to draw 6-6 in the Football League – on Monday 21 April 1930 at Filbert Street,.

Arsenal are the only club to have a London Underground Tube station named after them (formerly Gillespie Road) and the only team in the 20th Century to reach three successive FA Cup Finals.

Arsène Wenger is the only foreign manager to have won the double (1998 and 2002). His assistant Pat Rice is the only man to have won the double as a player (1971) and as a member of coaching staff (1998, 2002).

Arsenal are the only club to have scored in every Premiership game in a season (2001-02) and also the only club go to an entire Premiership season unbeaten (2003-2004). Thierry Henry is the only player ever to have won the Football Writers' Association Player of the Year three times.

THE ONLY FOREIGN MANAGER TO HAVE WON THE DOUBLE

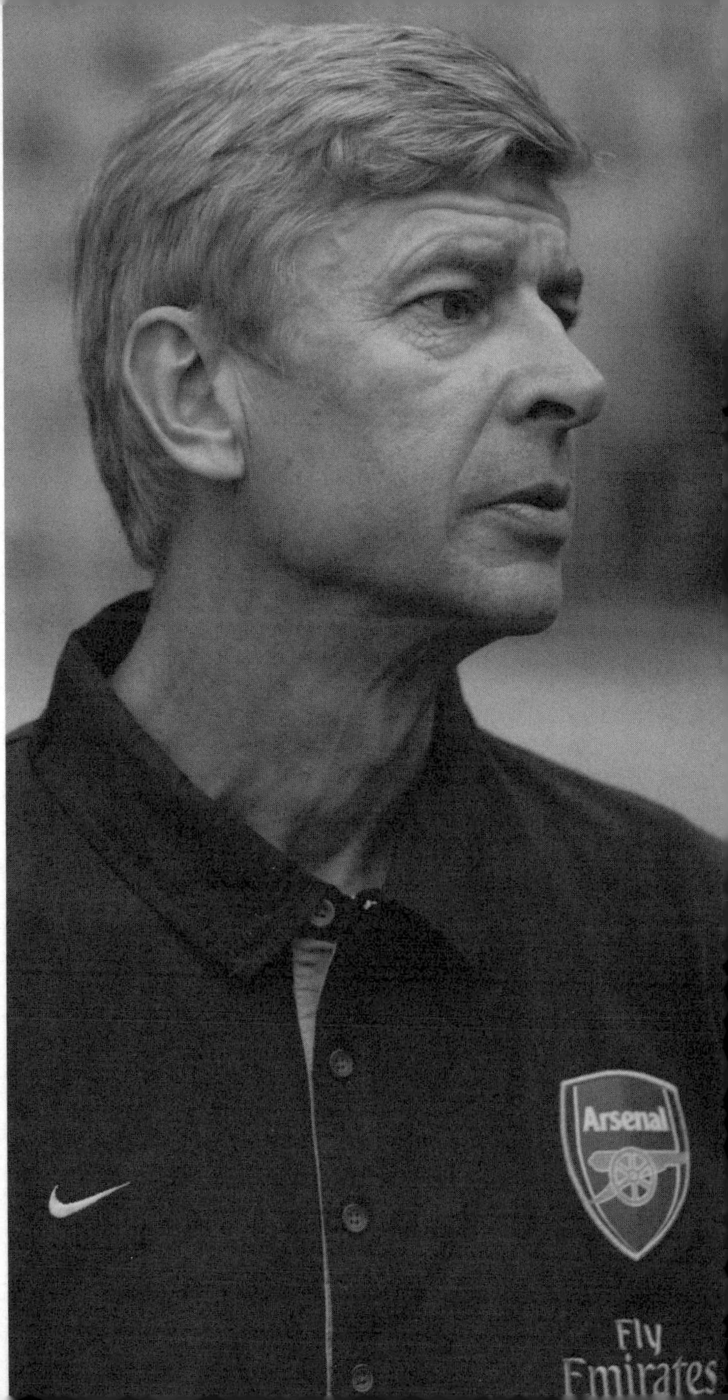

UP FOR THE CUP – XXVII

Arsenal 0 Manchester United 0 (5-4 on penalties)

On Saturday 21 May 2005, Arsenal played Manchester United in the FA Cup Final, again at the Millennium Stadium. Many Manchester United fans wore black in protest of their club being bought by American tycoon Malcolm Glazer. Near the end José Antonio Reyes was sent off. After 120 goalless minutes, the match went to penalties and Arsenal ran out 5-4 winners. Arsenal: Jens Lehmann, Lauren, Ashley Cole, Gilberto, Kolo Touré, Philippe Senderos, Patrick Vieira, Cesc Fàbregas (Robin van Persie), Robert Pirès (Edu) , Dennis Bergkamp (Freddie Ljungberg), José Antonio Reyes.

THE ARSENAL – DECADE BY DECADE: 2000s

2000-01

Premier League	P	W	D	L	F	A	W	D	L	F	A	Pts
2. Arsenal	38	15	3	1	45	13	5	7	7	18	25	70

FA Cup: Runners-up

League Cup: Third round   Europe: UCL Quarter-final

2001-02

Premier League	P	W	D	L	F	A	W	D	L	F	A	Pts
1. Arsenal	38	12	4	3	42	25	14	5	0	37	11	87

FA Cup: Winners

League Cup: Fifth round   Europe: ECL Second phase

2002-03

Premier League	P	W	D	L	F	A	W	D	L	F	A	Pts
2. Arsenal	38	15	2	2	47	20	8	7	4	38	22	78

FA Cup: Winners

League Cup: Third round   Europe: ECL Second phase

2003-04

Premier League	P	W	D	L	F	A	W	D	L	F	A	Pts
1. Arsenal	38	15	4	0	40	14	11	8	0	33	12	90

FA Cup: Semi-final

League Cup: Semi-final   Europe: ECL Quarter-final

2004-05

Premier League	P	W	D	L	F	A	W	D	L	F	A	Pts
2. Arsenal	38	13	5	1	54	19	12	3	4	33	17	83

FA Cup: Winners
League Cup: Quarter-final   Europe: ECL Round of 16

2005-06

Premier League	P	W	D	L	F	A	W	D	L	F	A	Pts
4. Arsenal	38	14	3	2	48	13	6	4	9	20	18	67

FA Cup: Fourth round
League Cup: Semi-final   Europe: ECL Runners-up

2006-07

Premier League	P	W	D	L	F	A	W	D	L	F	A	Pts
4. Arsenal	38	12	6	1	43	16	7	5	7	20	19	68

FA Cup: Fifth round
League Cup: Runners-up   Europe: ECL Round of 16

2007-08

Premier League	P	W	D	L	F	A	W	D	L	F	A	Pts
3. Arsenal	38	14	5	0	37	11	10	6	3	37	20	83

FA Cup: Fifth round
League Cup: Semi-final   Europe: ECL Quarter-final

THE INVINCIBLES

In 2003-04 Arsenal went an entire season unbeaten – just as manager Arsène Wenger had predicted they would. Before and after that season Arsenal had had an unbeaten run – between 7 May 2003 (Arsenal 6 Southampton 1) and 16 October 2004 (Arsenal 3 Aston Villa 1) they were undefeated for 49 glorious games. Five Arsenal players appeared in 41 or more matches of that run – with Thierry Henry and Kolo Touré missing just one game each!

48 games .... Thierry Henry, Kolo Touré
47 games .... Jens Lehmann
45 games .... Robert Pirès
41 games .... Ashley Cole

THEY DIED TOO YOUNG

Terry Anderson

Anderson signed pro terms in August 1961. He won two England youth caps but found it difficult to break into the side on a regular basis. Anderson made his first team debut in a 4–0 win over West Ham United on 2 March 1963. He had made just 25 appearances (scoring six goals) before leaving the club for Norwich City in February 1965 for a £15,000 fee, a record at that time for a winger. He retired in May 1976, but on Saturday 5 January 1980, he drowned, aged 35, during a training run in Yarmouth.

Walter Anderson

A forward, he played 27 times and hit the back of the net ten times. After 18 months at Arsenal he left for Plymouth Argyle in June 1903. He was still with the Pilgrims when he died in March 1904, aged just 25.

Spencer Bassett

Joined Woolwich Arsenal as an amateur in July 1906 but his appearances were limited. On 9 April 1917, he died in France of wounds received in the First World War. He was 31.

Bob Benson

Benson joined Woolwich Arsenal on 18 November 1913 from Sheffield United for a fee of £200. A full-back, on occasion he played as a centre-forward and was a killer penalty taker, with an 80-yard run-up! He played over 50 times for Arsenal, and scored twice on his last game, a 7–0 win over Nottingham Forest in the last game of the 1914-15 season. On 19 February 1916, he was at Highbury to watch his former club play Reading. Arsenal were a man short – Benson's former full-back colleague Joe Shaw could not get permission from the munitions factory to play. Benson stepped into the breach. It was the first time he had played in more than a year and his lack of match fitness showed. During the second half, he collapsed with exhaustion on the pitch. He staggered to the bench and trainer George Hardy helped him to the dressing room, but Benson died in the trainer's arms, aged just 33. He was buried in his Arsenal shirt. Three months later, Arsenal played a Rest of London Combination team in a testimonial (the first of its kind) for Benson's widow before a crowd of more than 5,000. His death was later ascribed to a burst blood vessel.

James Blair

Born in Scotland, inside forward Jimmy Blair signed for Arsenal in May 1905 for a fee of £500 from Kilmarnock. He scored on his debut the following September in a 3-1 win over Liverpool. He made just 13 first-team appearances and scored three times before being sold to Manchester City for £150 in November 1906. Six years later, after playing for Bradford City and Stockport County, he returned to his home in Dumfries. On 12 March 1913, Blair killed himself. He was 27.

Charles Booth

An outside-left, Charlie Booth signed for Arsenal in August 1892 and was in the side for the very first league match against Newcastle United. He played 16 times for Arsenal before moving to Loughborough Town in August 1894. He died in Leicester on 11 September 1898, aged just 29.

Bob Buchanan

An inside-forward and Scottish international, Bob Buchanan joined Woolwich Arsenal in September 1894. At the club, he averaged a goal every three games and scored nine in his first season. He died in Woolwich in December 1907, aged just 38.

Tommy Caton

Tommy Caton joined Arsenal on Thursday 1 December 1983 from Manchester City for £500,000 following the Maine Road club's relegation. The centre-half made his debut two days later at home to West Bromwich Albion in a 1-0 defeat. Caton became a mainstay in the defence alongside David O'Leary for two years. Caton lost his place to Tony Adams and Martin Keown and was sold to Oxford United in February 1987. He played 95 times for Arsenal scoring three times. Six years later, on 30 April 1993, he died of a heart attack brought on by years of alcoholism which led to him drinking two bottles of gin a day. Tommy Caton was just 30.

Peter Connolly

Born in Kirkcaldy, Fife in 1867, he played for Kirkcaldy Wanderers before joining Arsenal at the end of 1888. Connolly made his debut for the club on Saturday 5 October 1889 against Lyndhurst. Unusually, Connolly could either play as a full-back or as a centre-forward. Peter Connolly died on Thursday 12 September 1895, aged only 28.

Bobby Daniel

The elder brother of Ray Daniel, Bobby was killed in an RAF bombing raid in 1943. He was only 18.

Jack Lambert

In June 1926, Herbert Chapman signed centre-forward Lambert from Doncaster Rovers for £2,000. On Monday 6 September 1926, Lambert made his debut against Bolton Wanderers at Burnden Park but it was not for four more years that he became a regular. In the 1929-30 season, he scored 18 times in 20 matches and a goal in the 1930 FA Cup final. The next season, he scored 38 goals in 34 league games including seven hat-tricks. In October 1933, he was sold to Fulham and stayed at Craven Cottage for two years. In 1936, he became coach of Margate, Arsenal's nursery club. Two years later, he returned to Arsenal as reserve team coach. However, before he had the chance to see his protégés move into the first team he was killed in a car accident in December 1940 at Enfield, Middlesex. He was 38.

Jack McClelland

Intended as the replacement for Jack Kelsey, McClelland started well but broke a collarbone and soon found he was fighting for the number one jersey with Jim Furnell. McClelland left for Fulham in December 1964. He died of cancer on 15 March 1976, aged just 35.

Hugh McDonald

One of the few players to play for Arsenal on three separate occasions, McDonald was a useful goalie. He died on 27 August 1920, aged 36.

Joe Powell

A fine full-back, Joe Powell was serving in the Army when Arsenal signed him in December 1892. In 1893-94, he became the club's first captain in league football and missed just two games that season. The next year, he missed just three matches and in 1895-96, he missed five games out of 30 and scored his only goal in a 5-0 victory against Loughborough Town on 4 January 1896. He started in eight of the first 10 matches of the 1896-97 season but he fell awkwardly while playing Kettering Town on 23 November 1896 and broke his arm. Powell came down with tetanus and blood poisoning. The arm was amputated but he died six days later. He was just 26.

Sidney Pugh

A wing-half, he joined Arsenal in 1936. In April 1944, he was killed in action during the Second World War. He was 24.

Charlie Randall

Centre-forward Randall was killed in action on 27 September 1916 in France. He was 34.

Herbie Roberts

Right-half Roberts joined Arsenal from Oswestry Town in December 1926 for £200 and made his debut in a 3-2 win against Aston Villa on Monday 18 April 1927. He struggled to find a place in the first team and in his first two seasons played just five games. Manager Herbert Chapman moved Roberts to the centre of defence to counter the relaxation of the offside law. After missing the 1930 FA Cup Final through injury, Roberts became a stalwart in the side for six years winning an FA Cup winners' and four Championship medals. He represented England once against Scotland on Saturday 28 March 1931. Playing against Middlesbrough on Saturday 30 October 1937, he broke a leg and was forced into retirement. Although Arsenal won another League title that year, Roberts had only played in 13 games, one fewer than needed to get a winner's medal. Having played 333 games and scored five goals, he became Arsenal's reserve team trainer. On the outbreak of the Second World War, he joined the Royal Fusiliers as a lieutenant. On Monday 19 June 1944, Roberts died from erysipelas – an acute bacterial infection of the skin – at the age of 39. Tom Whittaker said, "Roberts's genius came from his intelligence and, even more important, he did what he was told."

David Rocastle

Rocky was one of Arsenal's most popular players in the Eighties and Nineties. He joined the club in 1983 and made 218 appearances for the club until he left in 1992. He signed for Leeds United for £2million and played for five more teams before his retirement in 1999. In February 2001, Rocastle announced that he was suffering from non-Hodgkin's lymphoma. Despite chemotherapy Rocastle died on Saturday 31 March 2001, aged 33. Later that day, Arsenal played Spurs at Highbury and in Rocastle's memory beat the Lillywhites 2-0, the first goal coming from Robert Pirès wearing Rocky's old number seven shirt.

Dicky Roose

Dr Roose replaced George Burdett as goalie. He was 38 when killed in action on 7 October 1916, serving with the 9th Battalion Royal Fusiliers.

Harry Storer

Another goalie that died young, Storer spent just over 18 months with Woolwich Arsenal. He died at Holloway, Derbyshire, on 25 April 1908 from consumption. He was 37.

Bobby Templeton

An outside-left, he cost Woolwich Arsenal £375 when signed from Aston Villa in December 1904. He won 11 caps for Scotland. He died of heart failure on 2 November 1919 after catching the flu during the epidemic that swept Europe after the First World War. He was 40.

Harry Thorpe

A left-back, he was in the team that won promotion to the First Division in 1903. In March 1908, he caught the flu while playing and died on 16 September 1908, aged just 28.

Ernie Tuckett

He died in May 1945 in France, aged just 31.

Paul Vaessen

Centre-forward Paul Vaessen made his debut aged 16 against Lokomotive Leipzig in the Uefa Cup in September 1978. His league debut came eight months later against Chelsea. On Wednesday 23 April 1980, he had his greatest moment when he scored against Juventus in Turin, in the second leg of the European Cup Winners' Cup semi-final before 66,386 fans. Vaessen replaced David Price in the 75th minute and, with two minutes to go scored the most important goal of his career. It was the first time any British team had won at Juventus. Vaessen's career suffered through injury and he was forced to retire from the game in the summer of 1983, aged 21, having scored nine goals in 39 games. The club did little for Vaessen after retirement. He did a number of menial jobs, but unable to cope, became a heroin addict. An attempt to train as a physiotherapist ended in failure and on Wednesday 8 August 2001, he was found dead in his bathroom in Henbury, Bristol, a large amount of drugs in his bloodstream. He was 39.

UP FOR THE CUP – XXVIII

Arsenal 1 Barcelona 2

On Wednesday 17 May 2006, Arsenal appeared in their first-ever European Cup Final, at the Stade de France in Paris. After 18 minutes, Jens Lehmann became the first player to be sent off in the final, for a professional foul on Samuel Eto'o. Arsène Wenger withdrew Robert Pirès, much to the player's upset, and replaced him with reserve keeper Manuel Almunia. Ten-man Arsenal scored first in the 37th minute: Sol Campbell got his head on the end of a Thierry Henry free kick, but Barcelona made their superior numbers felt. Eto'o equalised in the 76th minute, and four minutes later, sub Juliano Belletti hit the winner for the Spaniards. Thierry Henry said, "They kicked me all over the place but I was the one who got a yellow card. No disrespect to Barcelona but we were the better team when it was 11 v 11." The next day, the referee Terje Hauge admitted that he had made a mistake in sending off Lehmann. Arsenal: Jens Lehmann, Emmanuel Eboué, Ashley Cole, Gilberto, Kolo Touré, Sol Campbell, Cesc Fàbregas (Matthieu Flamini), Alexander Hleb (José Antonio Reyes), Robert Pirès (Manuel Almunia), Thierry Henry (captain), Freddie Ljungberg.

UP FOR THE CUP – XXIX

Arsenal 1 Chelsea 2

The fifth League Cup Final involving the Gunners, on Sunday 25 February 2007 at the Millennium Stadium, was the first all-London League Cup Final. Arsenal led after 11 minutes, Theo Walcott with his first goal for the club. Eight minutes later, Didier Drogba equalised for Chelsea – his 27th goal of the season. After 84 minutes Drogba headed Chelsea into the lead. Seven minutes of stoppage time were added, due to an injury to John Terry, and in the 96th minute a brawl resulted in red cards for Arsenal's Kolo Touré and Chelsea's Mikel John Obi; substitute Emmanuel Adebayor was also sent off. Arsène Wenger said, "It suddenly exploded. It was strange as it didn't reflect the quality of the game. Suddenly we lost it and they lost it as well and it became a brawl." The full-time whistle eventually blew in the 103rd minute of play. Arsenal: Manuel Almunia, Justin Hoyte, Abou Diaby (Alexander Hleb), Cesc Fàbregas, Kolo Touré (captain), Philippe Senderos, Júlio Baptista, Denílson, Jérémie Aliadière (Emmanuel Adebayor), Theo Walcott, Armand Traoré (Emmanuel Eboué).

ARSENAL BAD BOYS

Tony Adams

Tony Adams was born on Monday 10 October 1966 in Romford, Essex and signed for Arsenal as a schoolboy in 1980. He made his first team debut on Saturday 5 November 1983 at Highbury in a 2-1 defeat by Sunderland. On Friday 1 January 1988, he became Arsenal's captain, a job he would hold for the next 14 years. Adams was a fighter for the club on the pitch and increasingly became a brawler in nightclubs. On Sunday 6 May 1990, he was due to meet his team mates at Highbury to go off on tour but decided to have one for the road at a party in Braintree and somehow ended up at a barbecue in Rainham. At 3pm Adams thought it was about time he joined his team mates so he jumped into his Ford Sierra to drive to Heathrow. At 80mph Adams lost control and crashed into a garden demolishing the front wall. When he was breathalysed, Adams was found to be more than four times over the legal drink-drive limit. The police allowed Adams to join the Arsenal team and a friend drove him to Heathrow where he boarded a plane for the 13-hour flight to Singapore. On Wednesday 19 December 1990, Adams appeared at Southend Crown Court where he was jailed for four months. He served half of his sentence (57 days) at Chelmsford Prison as prisoner LE1561 and was freed on Friday 15 February 1991. The following day, as the first team played Leeds United in an FA Cup replay, Adams turned out for the reserves in a 2-2 draw against Reading. On the outside, Adams continued to drink and often played with a hangover. On Sunday 28 February 1993, Adams and some friends went to Towcester racecourse. Afterwards they went to a nightclub where Adams fell down a flight of concrete stairs necessitating 29 stitches in a head wound. A week later, Arsenal beat Ipswich Town 4-2 at Portman Road in the FA Cup Quarter Final; Adams was man of the match! In October that year, with Ray Parlour, Adams let off a fire extinguisher in a Pizza Hut in Hornchurch, Essex, after Spurs fans taunted the pair. Finally, on Saturday 14 September 1996, Adams admitted to the public that he was an alcoholic. It was thanks to the regime introduced by Arsène Wenger who joined the club shortly after that Adams extended his career and became the only player in English football history to have captained a League-winning team in three different decades.

Marcus Artry

On Friday 7 November 2003, Artry, a promising youth team player who had been with the club for eight years and had represented England at under-18 level, was sent to prison for nine years for his part in three vicious group sex attacks on women and girls as young as 14. The attacks by the gang of four – Artry, 18-year-old Kyle Reid and a 17-year-old and 14-year-old, who were not named for legal reasons – took place between March 2002 and 8 February 2003. Artry was convicted of one charge of rape, one of indecent assault and one of indecency with a child.

Steve Burtenshaw

Coach, chief scout, caretaker manager – Burtenshaw served Arsenal in many roles. In 1992 he received £35,000 from agent Rune Hauge following Danish midfielder John Jensen's move from Brondby to Arsenal. Burtenshaw stayed at the club until Bruce Rioch was sacked on Monday 12 August 1996. On Thursday 24 September 1998, Burtenshaw was fined £7,500 and £2,500 costs by the Football Association for his part in the bungs scandal. By that time, he had followed Rioch and Stewart Houston to Loftus Road where he worked as chief scout for Queens Park Rangers.

Paul Davis

Paul Davis was a loyal servant to the club whose loyalty was not always adequately rewarded. In 1988, he was fined £3,000 and banned for nine games after he was found guilty by television of breaking Glen Cockerill's jaw during a match against Southampton on Saturday 17 September 1988. Neither the referee nor either of his linesmen had seen the incident.

Kevin Dennis

In September 1993, reserve Kevin Dennis was sentenced to 30 months for manslaughter. At his initial hearing, Arsenal's lawyers, showing admirable loyalty to an employee, asked the magistrate if the case could be brought forward as they had a car waiting outside to take the player down to a reserve match. In December 1999, 23-year-old Batatunde Oba was murdered near the Broadway Boulevard nightclub in Ealing, west London. On Monday 18 December 2000 at the Old Bailey, Dennis, his brother, Desmond, and two relatives, Carl Dennis and Stefan Williams, were found guilty of the murder. Mr Oba was stabbed nine times in the back of the head, chest, stomach, arms and legs. It took seven bouncers to stop the attack.

Charlie George

The hero of the North Bank failed to achieve too much after his magnificent double-winning goal in the 1971 FA Cup Final and soon left Highbury for Derby County. He is now a guide at the Arsenal Museum. It is surprising but George won just one cap for England. Alf Ramsey snubbed him and Don Revie seemed to do the same. In 1976, Revie finally picked George and he played for 60 minutes against the Republic of Ireland. Would Revie have picked him again? We will never know because after he was subbed, the England manager asked George if he wanted to sit on the bench or go for a bath and George told his boss to "go fuck yourself". In 1978, he was fined £440 for assaulting Jack Spencer, a journalist with *The Eastern Daily Press*. George later commented, "It was the stupidest thing I ever did, but it was totally out of character. I sometimes wonder if I'm remembered more for that than my goal for Arsenal in the Cup Final."

George Graham

In 1992, Graham met Norwegian football agent Rune Hauge at a London hotel. Subsequently, he signed Pal Lydersen and John Jensen and in the process received a bung of £425,000 – or as Graham put it "unsolicited gifts". In 1995, the FA began an investigation into transfers and the payments were revealed. Arsenal sacked Graham on 21 February and the FA banned him from football for a year. Graham called Arsenal's decision "a kangaroo-court judgment". In the autumn of 1998, he became manager of Spurs.

Perry Groves

In 1990, Groves was fined two weeks' wages along with Nigel Winterburn, Paul Merson and Kevin Richardson for drinking before a key game. At 1.15am on 26 April 2008, Groves was arrested in Crouch Street, Colchester for being abusive. A police spokesman said, "Police issued a 43-year-old man from Colchester with a fixed penalty notice for a Section 5 public order offence of using abusive and insulting words and behaviour, likely to cause harassment."

David Hillier

Hillier joined Arsenal in January 1984 as an associated schoolboy. He later became a trainee and turned professional in February 1988. Hillier was captain when Arsenal beat Doncaster Rovers in the 1988 FA Youth Cup final. He made his first-team debut on Tuesday 25 September 1990 in the League Cup against Chester City in the first leg 1-0 win. He became a semi-regular midfielder for the club but missed the 1993 League Cup and FA Cup finals and the 1994 European Cup Winners' Cup Final through injury. In March 1995, during a drugs test at the Arsenal training ground Hillier tested positive for cannabis but said he had accidentally smoked a spiked cigarette at a party. In January 1996, Hillier appeared in court accused of stealing luggage worth £3,000 at Gatwick Airport. He was fined £750. When Arsène Wenger became manager, Hillier's days at the club were numbered and he was sold to Portsmouth.

George Jobey

The first man to score for Woolwich Arsenal at Highbury went into management when he retired. In May 1941, while in charge at Notts County, he was banned for life from football after being found guilty in an investigation into illegal payments paid between 1925 and 1938 (when he was manager of Derby County). The ban was lifted in 1945 and he died 17 years later.

Gerrit Keizer (also Keyser)

The first foreign player to play for Arsenal, he joined the club in 1930, aged 19, even though he was still technically on the books of Ajax. He said that he came to England to improve his English. He made his debut in the 4-1 victory against Blackpool at Bloomfield Road on 30 August 1930. He kept goal for the first dozen games that season. On Saturdays, he would play for Arsenal and then fly back to Holland that night to play for Ajax the next day earning him the nickname The Flying Dutchman. As with many of his ilk, Keizer's performances ranged from the erratic to the brilliant. Arsenal's other keepers Charlie Preedy and Bill Harper kept him on his toes and Herbert Chapman eventually tired of the young Dutchman. He dropped Keizer in October and never picked him for the first team again. In July 1931, Keizer moved to Charlton Athletic. He continued to shuttle between London and Amsterdam ostensibly bringing football kits with him. In 1947, Dutch customs officers discovered that he was also importing British bank notes, then an offence. He was fined 30,000 guilders and given a six-month prison sentence. Out of jail, he started a successful greengrocery business and in 1955 became a director of Ajax. He died on 5 December 1980.

Malcom Macdonald and Alan Hudson

Two of Terry Neill's signings, sadly they had no respect for the genial Irishman. On a tour of the Far East and Australia in the summer of 1977, the team arrived in Singapore and the players asked for £800 spending money, but were upset to be offered just £6 a day. The team were scheduled to attend a function with officials from Singapore and the British Embassy, but after half an hour Macdonald and Hudson walked out. The next day, Terry Neill laid into them telling them that they had embarrassed the club. Two days later, on 12 July 1977, Arsenal played Red Star Belgrade and lost 2-1 (Macdonald got the goal). The players lost around eight pints of fluid during the match and a local Australian doctor suggested that they replaced the liquid by drinking water or beer! Offering beer as a solution to dehydration was probably not what the doctor should have ordered, but the players took him at his word. Arsenal beat Singapore 5-1 on 16 July with Macdonald hitting a hat-trick and the team flew to Sydney. Malcolm Macdonald claimed that he was given a child's bed at the Rushcutters Hotel – Hudson said it would have suited Ronnie Corbett! Arsenal played an Australian National XI on 20 July and lost 3-1 and then went down to Celtic 3-2 on 24 July at the Sydney Cricket Ground. Terry Neill banned the players from drinking but they ignored him. George Armstrong joined Hudson and Macdonald on a drinking spree. On their return to the hotel, Arsenal chairman Denis Hill-Wood bought Macdonald a gin and tonic in the hotel bar. Then Macdonald and Hudson both took sleeping pills and went to bed. Unfortunately, Terry Neill had arranged a training session and sent club captain Pat Rice to their rooms to rouse the two sleeping players. It was too much for Terry Neill and he sent Hudson and Macdonald home. Liam Brady later admitted that at least ten other players should also have been sent home for the same "offence". Back in England Hudson never played for Arsenal again – he was sold to Seattle Sounders for £100,000 – but Macdonald and Neill made their peace.

Paul Merson

Born in London on 20 March 1968, Paul Merson joined Arsenal as an apprentice in 1984 and signed professional terms on 1 December 1985. After a loan spell at Brentford, he made his debut for the Gunners on 22 November 1986 against Manchester City in a 3-0 win at Highbury. Merson became a stalwart of the Arsenal side in the 1990s and won the PFA Young Player of the Year award. On Wednesday 11 September 1991, he made his full England debut, playing against Germany. Three years later, on Friday 25 November 1994, Merson confessed to being an alcoholic and cocaine addict. The FA sorted a three-month rehab program for him and Merson returned to the Arsenal side as a substitute in a nil-nil draw against AC Milan on 1 February 1995, just before George Graham was sacked. Arsenal continued to pay his £5,000-a-week wages while he was in rehab. He said, "I've stayed away from drink and drugs but gambling has beat me, spanked me all over the place. This is one of the biggest killers in the world. Every day it would go through my head about committing suicide." Manager Stewart Houston kept faith with the player and kept Merson in the side, as did his successors Bruce Rioch and Arsène Wenger. On 7 July 1997, Wenger sold Merson to Middlesbrough for £5million. In all Merson played 423 times for Arsenal, scoring 99 goals. He won two championship medals at Highbury as well as FA Cup, League Cup and European Cup Winners' Cup honours. In 2003 he was held by the police for five hours after allegedly assaulting his wife. Merson recalled, "The last thing a policeman said to me when I left the cell was, 'People would give their right arm to be like you.' I said, 'I'd give my right arm just to be normal.'" In February 2004, he admitted himself to the Sierra Tucson Clinic in Arizona to seek help for his gambling addiction.

Sammy Nelson

The full-back was suspended by Arsenal after a home game with Coventry City on 3 April 1979. Having scored an own goal, Nelson pulled one back for Arsenal and celebrated by flashing his backside to the North Bank.

Charlie Nicholas

'Champagne Charlie' joined Arsenal from Celtic in June 1983 for £750,000. He quickly made more headlines for his off-pitch activities than what he did in the famous red and white. He dated the beautiful gymnast Suzanne Dando and claimed that he ended the relationship because she liked seeing her face in the tabloids a little too often for his liking! Singer Thereza Bazar from pop duo Dollar sold a kiss'n'tell to the *News of the World*. She pointedly noted that despite problems scoring on the pitch Nicholas had scored a hat-trick with her. In the space of four years, he was twice charged with drink driving. On one occasion, Nicholas tried to disguise his inebriation by zigzagging home at a careful 10mph. He received a three-year ban and was sold to Aberdeen on Thursday 7 January 1988 for £400,000.

Sir Henry Norris

Manager Hebert Chapman told Norris, the first football tsar, that he needed to spend money to make the club successful. In 1925 Chapman arranged to buy Charlie Buchan who was worth £5,000. Norris arranged to pay Sheffield United £2,000 up front plus £100 for every goal Buchan scored in the first season. For some reason, there was month-long delay in the deal. In 1927, the *Daily Mail* ran a series of articles alleging that Norris was guilty of making illegal payments to Buchan. That same year, Norris also sold the team bus for £125 and the money ended up in his wife's bank account. Norris sued the Mail in 1927 claiming that as he had invested £125,000 in the club he was entitled to £125. In court, Norris tried to bring down Herbert Chapman with him. (In 1919, Chapman and the directors of Leeds United had been accused of making illegal payments and Chapman was suspended. He successfully appealed and returned as manager of Huddersfield Town.) The judge found for the newspaper and Norris sued the FA. In February 1929 the Lord Chief Justice found for the FA, and they banned Norris for life from football. In 1928, it was alleged that Norris had told Arsenal to take it easy against Manchester United and Portsmouth so that struggling Spurs were relegated. Nothing was proved but such was Norris's reputation at the time that it was generally believed. As Arsenal began to gain honours in the 1930s Norris was forced to watch from the stands. He died from a massive heart attack at his home, Sirron Lodge, Barnes Common, London SW13 on 30 July 1934, six months after Herbert Chapman. He left £72,051 4s. 1d (the equivalent of around £1million in 2008). Norris bequeathed £100 to Leslie Knighton, the manager he sacked to be replaced by Herbert Chapman.

Ray Parlour

Parlour joined Arsenal as a trainee in 1989, and signed professional terms on Wednesday 6 March 1991. He made his debut for the Gunners at Anfield in a 2-0 defeat against Liverpool on Wednesday 29 January 1992, where he conceded a penalty. Parlour became a first-team regular in the 1994-95 season, the year that he was questioned by police after a fight at Butlins in Bognor Regis. On another occasion Parlour was questioned by police in Hong Kong after he threw a packet of prawn crackers into a taxi. The driver, Lai-Pak Yan, chased the Arsenal player with a wooden club so Parlour whacked him one on the nose. On Friday 23 July 2004, he signed for Middlesbrough.

Jermaine Pennant

Pennant joined Arsenal from Notts County in 1999 for £2 million, a record fee for a trainee at the time and looked a likely Arsenal great for the future. Off and on the field he was troubled. England under-21 coach Howard Wilkinson sent Pennant home for bad behaviour and then the player was sent off for punching an opponent in a match against Croatia. He made his Arsenal debut aged 16 years and 319 days on 30 November 1999 in the League Cup defeat by Middlesbrough. He did not make his league debut until 24 August 2002 when he played against West Ham United as a substitute. Pennant's attitude had not improved and he was often late for training much to the annoyance of Arsène Wenger. Eventually, the manager lost patience with him and loaned Pennant to Birmingham City for the 2004-05 season. On 23 January 2005, Pennant crashed his Mercedes into a lamppost in Aylesbury while driving drunk, uninsured and serving a 16-month driving ban. When the police arrived to arrest him, Pennant told them he was Ashley Cole. Tests showed Pennant's alcohol reading was 85 micrograms per 100ml of breath. The legal limit is 35 micrograms. On 1 March, Pennant was sentenced to 90 days in prison but released on parole after 30 days on condition he wore an electronic tag at all times – even on the pitch. In April 2005, Pennant signed permanently for Birmingham.

Graham Rix

The curly-headed midfielder replaced Arsenal legend George Armstrong on the left wing. Rix made his debut for the club and scored his first goal against Leicester City on Saturday 2 April 1977. He became a club hero with his cross to Alan Sunderland in the 1979 FA Cup Final, which resulted in the winning goal. The following year, his penalty miss handed the European Cup Winners' Cup to Valencia. In 1983, Rix was appointed club captain but was unable to lead the team to any silverware. Injuries forced him out of the side and he lost his place to Martin Hayes before leaving for the French side Caen. His last Arsenal appearance was in the League in a 2–1 win against Everton on Saturday 7 May 1988. In all he played 464 times for the Gunners, scoring 51 goals. On retirement, he joined Chelsea's coaching staff and even played once for them in the Premier League in May 1995 during an injury crisis – ironically against Arsenal. On Friday 26 March 1999, at Knightsbridge Crown Court Rix was sentenced to 12 months in prison for having underage sex with a 15-year-old girl and indecently assaulting her. Rix was believed to have met the girl and had sex with her at a west London hotel on the eve of Chelsea's Premier League match with Manchester United in February 1998. Passing sentence, the judge said, "These offences took place when she was only weeks short of her 16th birthday, the age of consent, yet at the time of the offences she was a virgin, plainly a girl who was undoubtedly like any other fascinated and flattered by the attentions of a man who was to her knowledge a celebrity, attended by the glamour of fame and success. There was in my view a significant amount of irresponsibility in your behaviour, illustrating a determination to have sex irrespective of her feelings." He served six months of his sentence and, on release, was placed on the sex offenders' register for 10 years. Chelsea gave him his old job back.

Kenny Sansom

After joining from Crystal Palace, Sansom made his Arsenal debut against West Bromwich Albion on Saturday 16 August 1980 in a 1-0 win at the Hawthorns. Sansom was ever present that season and the next, making the number three shirt his own. In 1981, he was voted Arsenal's Player of the Year. Six years later, he was captain when Arsenal won the League Cup beating Liverpool 2-1. The next season, George Graham replaced Sansom as captain with 21-year-old Tony Adams. Although Kenny Sansom was a popular and hard-working player, off the field he had problems. Terry Neill who signed him said that the defender "had inflated expectations of what a million pound footballer earns". Sansom then lived near Arsenal's training ground at London Colney and bought himself a Jaguar for the short journey to the ground. Again Terry Neill, "He probably didn't get it out of second gear. In his position he'd have been better off getting himself a push bike." Cars were not Sansom's vice – gambling was and alcohol was not too far behind. His drinking became so bad that at one time his daughter, Natalie, wrapped up her baby, put her in a buggy and searched every pub in town until she found her errant father, alone with only a bottle of wine for company. Sansom blamed his father, a south London ducker and diver for getting him into drink. He recalls, "At night we would hit Langan's, Tramp or Stringfellows. I acquired the nickname Mr Chablis because of my liking for white wine. After I joined Arsenal from Palace, I would drive back from training, stopping at a bookie's along the way, placing bets and having a drink. At first, gambling was more important, but as time went on I fell further and further into alcoholism. I never knew I was becoming an alcoholic. I wasn't drinking any more than my team mates. My gambling addiction was part of my journey into alcoholism. My wife, Elaine, won £800 at bingo. I blew the lot on a horse that lost. When I got home, I locked myself in the bathroom, refusing to come out. I swore I would never gamble again, but I could not stop myself." Before the League Cup Final against Luton Town, George Graham arranged for the team to go to Marbella for a bonding trip. On the day the team was due to leave, Sansom arrived home at 3am very drunk. Sansom again, "I refused to go but, once Graham was informed, he sent word I had to catch them up or I wouldn't play in the final. I flew out as soon as possible and was still drunk as I wandered around Puerto Banus trying to discover which hotel Arsenal were staying in. After we lost to Luton at Wembley, I wished I hadn't bothered." In 1998, Sansom went bankrupt. It was only when Sansom attended Tony Adams's Sporting Chance clinic that he finally came to terms with his demons and that drinking seven bottles of wine a day was not beneficial to him or his family. It was too late for one and his wife left him.

Peter Storey

The midfield hard man – nicknamed Snouty – played 391 league games (and more than 800 in total) for Arsenal before moving to Fulham in 1977. In December of that year he was fined £65 after head butting a lollipop man who argued with him after Storey didn't stop at a pedestrian crossing. In 1979 he was fined £700 plus £175 costs and given a three-month suspended sentence for allowing three prostitutes to ply their trade from his rented flat in Leyton High Street, which was listed as the Calypso Massage Parlour. In 1980, Storey was jailed for three years at the Old Bailey for attempting to counterfeit gold coins. Two years later, he got two six-month sentences for car theft that had occurred in 1978. The sentences ran concurrently. In 1983, he was declared bankrupt and in 1990 received a 28-day prison sentence for illegally importing from France 14 pornographic videos. In 1991, he got a similar length sentence, albeit this time suspended, for swearing at a traffic warden.

Alan Sunderland

The scorer of the 1979 FA Cup winning goal killed two people in a road accident in July 1981 while driving along Bramley Road in Enfield, Middlesex after a charity cricket match at Cockfosters. He was found not guilty of driving without due care and attention but was banned for a year and fined £100.

Paul Vaessen

The triumph of 1980's European Cup Winners' Cup semi-final behind him, injury wrecked Paul Vaessen's career. "I was just 21," he told the *News Of The World*, "and, when the doors of Highbury shut behind me, I had no idea what to do... I was on the scrap heap." He became a drug addict taking heroin, cocaine and benzo-diazapan. He worked as a postman and on building sites but when he ran out of money he robbed warehouses and vans, and mugged people in the street to pay for his £125 a day habit. He became a regular in court often because he could not pay his fines. "I don't know how I stayed out of jail," he said. Vaessen was stabbed six times, from his armpit to his waist when a drugs deal went wrong in a side street off the Old Kent Road. Taken to Guy's Hospital, he "died" twice on the operating table. Convalescing, Vaessen booked himself out of the hospital and went in search of drugs. In May 1993, he admitted himself to a detox clinic in Bexleyheath for seven weeks. Five years later, Vaessen was charged with assaulting a policeman after stealing women's tights from Asda in Farnborough. As he was taken to the police van, Vaessen fell and a policeman grabbed him to stop him hitting the ground. Vaeesen then kicked him in the shin and said that the policeman had pushed him. In court, Vaessen's solicitor, Andrew Purkiss, told Aldershot magistrates, "This is a very tragic case. Twenty years ago, my client was on top of the world with everything to look forward to. However, at 21, doctors told him that he would be crippled if he played professional football again. His whole life was turned upside down and he was very desperate. In those days, there was no counselling or after-playing help and he was told by Arsenal, 'Goodbye and good luck'". Vaessen was sentenced to 90 days for assault, and was bailed on condition he lived at his brother's home in Henbury, north of Bristol. The conviction and sentence were later quashed on appeal. Three years later, Vaessen was dead.

Patrick Vieira

On 3 October 1999, he was sent off a 2-1 defeat at West Ham, for a foul on Paolo di Canio. As he left the pitch he spat at Neil Ruddock. The action resulted in him being fined £45,000 and banned for six matches. Vieira later said, "What I did was unforgivable... I'm a role model. My brother is a teacher. If one of his pupils spits at another, he can't tell him not to do it. The kids will just turn around and say, 'Your brother does exactly the same.' But the things that pisses me off is the £45,000 fine. Coming from where I do, I know the value of money. To my family, that is a phenomenal sum."